JEREMY HUGHES

I Found Rhode Island

Dedicated to
Benjamin Hardy Hughes,
Virgil Hardy Hughes Jr.,
and anyone else who has been led astray
by the deceptive promise of comfort from darkness.

This book has not been professionally proofread or edited. I didn't want it to be. I wanted this book to be as much of me as possible, maybe even with a few grammatical errors. I wanted it to be natural and raw. I didn't want my words, opinions, thoughts, or emotions to be altered or polished by someone who has not experienced what I have. I want you to be able to envision me and what I've been through by reading my own words. Besides, proofreading and editing cost too much.

J. Hughes

Foreword

Children should come with a handbook. Make that SEVERAL handbooks. They could be sorted chronologically, similar to how children are age-grouped into sports leagues. What to do with a newborn? There's a handbook for that! Toddlers? Look in the handbook! Youngsters? Pre-teens? Adolescents? Handbook, handbook, handbook! When your child reaches the age of 18, hardly the end of parenting, the manual is passed on to your child to keep and consult for all scenarios for the rest of their lives, especially when/if they have kids of their own.

Each generation could add notations, likely from their failures and weaknesses, to pass along the best wisdom available. It makes sense to me to have something to go by. Words of knowledge and love for the curators of the creations we bring into the world. Wouldn't it be neat to have someone to consult and, more importantly, someone to take responsibility when things go wrong? "But it was in the book; it wasn't me." Instead, we are somehow expected to make it work with our instincts and ragged memories of one's childhood. How hard can it be to see a child through until they can make it independently, anyway? Is it possible? Perhaps. But it would sure be easier with a book.

The book would say what to do in the case of potty training. "He won't do this!" The book would say, "When you face these circumstances, use this technique, and all will be well." Surely there is a handbook that states the correct way to navigate complex life choices. A handbook for parents to impart wisdom to their children when contemplating marriage, divorce, or enlisting in the U.S. Army. Just a little something to read when it feels as if everyone has let you go through life alone.

A handbook would surely be a better guide than an imperfect mother and a father who suffered from such curious illnesses. Perhaps with a manual, there would be less need for warning notes in this autobiography referencing the time "my father did this" or "my mother did that" along the way. But you the reader will not find a picture-book story free of missteps. Instead, you will be treated to an honest rendering of how this one person traversed the mental roller coaster of life. It is, most importantly, true. I would know. I was there from the beginning. I'm the mother who gave him life.

Jeremy Steven Hughes was born on April 11, 1978. Blond hair, blue-eyed, 21 inches long. Long and skinny but healthy. It was the frame of his father, who took after his mother's side of the family. Soaking wet, she did not weigh over 90 pounds. But this little boy barely weighed eight pounds when they laid him on my chest. He was so fragile and utterly dependent on those of us given the mission to nurture him. That day, I had no reason to suspect this child was different from any other child. He needed only the same fundamental upbringing as everyone else. He already had a brother, five years old, and in five more years, there would be another. He also had a half-brother and sister who were close.

Just make sure they're fed and clothed, patch up the skinned knees, and kiss the bumps and bruises away. Protect them like a mama grizzly and offer an occasional shoulder to cry on. Little did I know that a simple mother's love does not so easily whisk away some wounds. That would only become unavoidably obvious many years later. Perhaps it shouldn't have, but it came as a total surprise when the wheels suddenly, from my perspective, came off, and his life careened into a dark and dangerous place.

Jeremy was always more than a little curious. He wanted to know everything, especially if he got the sense that it was something he, perhaps, shouldn't. Quiet and shy, he preferred to stand away and assess things from the shadows. Until the pages of this book, I had no idea of the perceptions rattling around in his head, and I was amazed at the ones that went unchecked. While I obliviously sleepwalked through parenting, he was alert and attentive and processed everything. He was bright and curious, just not in the usual book-learning way. He did not do well or care to do well in school. We would learn he hated math and did not want numbers floating around in his head. He could not, and did not want to, tell you where any of them went. To him, they were just a big jumble of different colored shining stars that threatened to leave him screaming in torture. So, he avoided them whenever he could. Before he was eighteen, he received his GED and had one of the highest scores in his class. We did begin to have a bit of understanding at that time but still did not feel there was a major problem.

Jeremy did love working with his hands, taking things apart to see what makes them work, and then putting them back together again. In my view, that's precisely what this book is about. You are invited to journey along as Jeremy dismantles the details of his life and mind, examines them in the light of day and his current place of understanding, and then puts them back together. Hopefully, you will learn some hidden things about yourself along with him. It's not a manual, precisely because every journey is unique, but perhaps it will inspire us all to pay more attention to the critical pieces of the complex puzzle of a single solitary life and in this way perhaps we can walk more closely beside each other.

Preface

As far back as I can remember, I've always had to know the reason for my existence. Why I am here. What my purpose in life is. It's always been at the forefront of my mind. It's as if I have to know my purpose so I can make sure I don't fail at it. Whatever the case, determining my reason for being put on this planet has always been a daily goal. Some people never worry or think about this aspect of their lives. They just take each day as they come and whatever happens they assume is their purpose. I'm exactly the opposite.

As of the completion of this story, I am forty-five years old and have been officially diagnosed with mental illnesses for the last twenty-one years. Unfortunately, mental illness runs in the family, and it did not pass me over, at all. It hit me hard.

My bipolar depression took me to the darkest depths that I never imagined even existed. I've been balled up on the couch for days, crying non-stop, refusing to face the world. I've felt lost and helpless in a psychiatric unit numerous times. I've created a mask to cover up what was going on inside my mind. I've told people I was okay when I knew I wasn't. I've cast my depression aside simply because I didn't want to admit that I couldn't overcome it on my own.

My bipolar mania would take me on a crash course through six states, from Arizona all the way to Mississippi. The mania would sink its roots deep into my brain, gaining total control of my emotions and choices, and eventually gaining total control of every second and every aspect of my life. For ten days I would succumb to the power of this disorder. It would transform me into nothing more than a shell of a human. At the end of those ten days, I would have a total of nine felonies and four different law enforcement agencies searching for me.

This is the story of my struggle to find my purpose, while also struggling with mental illnesses.

(*50% of all proceeds benefit the North Little Rock, AR Fort Roots Veteran's Hospital 3K Psych Ward in providing reading material, activity items, pizza parties and such to patients.)

Head Cuffs

Its origins untraceable, but it's welcomed for the
companionship it provides.
There's no exit for its expansion. Behind your mind it breeds
and hides.
Inward it constricts every positive emotion you think you
own.
Fond memories with others drift away,
leaving you forever alone.
Surrendering seems easier than constructing another mask to
save face.
Tonight's worries about last night's worries keep you forever
awake.
You know not which mood you are ever actually in.
One doctor to the other all professing you'll eventually begin
again.
Comfortable with these depths, black seems a flower yellow.
Providing welcomed warmth until its penultimate bellow.
It's no longer just you. It's now the two of you.
Those overcome are prevalent.
Those cured are few.

-Jeremy S. Hughes

The License Plate Game

R ule #1: You cannot use the license plates of eighteen-wheelers.

Rule #2: You cannot use the license plates of the state you are currently driving in.

Living in central Arkansas and my mother living in west Tennessee, my two boys and I travel back and forth a lot for visits since it is only a two-hour drive one way. On one of these trips, we decided to keep track of all the license plates we would see along the way, just as a fun way to pass the time. To my surprise, this game turned quietness into conversation as my boys would ask questions about the states we would find. At age forty, you think you know a lot until your children start asking questions about the country you've lived in all your life. 'I'm not sure' and 'I don't know' were common replies during our travels. After so many questions, I would just tell them I didn't know the answer, even if I did, to avoid any drawn-out explanations.

The game always started the same, with the three of us looking at every car we passed or every car that passed us. Each of us wide-eyed trying to be the first to find a new plate. The entertainment would last thirty minutes or so and then the boys would become bored. They would start playing their games, fall asleep, or talk or argue with each other, leaving me to my mind for the rest of the ride. You can only keep young kids entertained for so long on a car trip. Don't worry, the older they get, the easier the trips get, I promise. Occasionally, to break the silence, I would yell out a license plate I saw even when I knew they were no longer paying attention.

Score it!

I know for a fact that my mind wanders and runs in an uncontrollably higher gear much more often than the average person. One second I'll be thinking about the ingredients of the drink in my cup holder, and the next second I will immediately divert my attention to my purpose in life. Why am I here? Why am I driving on this road at this very moment? Did I choose to be driving at this point in my life? Did someone or something else schedule this drive for me today? What the heck is sodium citrate and why is it in my Mountain Dew? Is it deadly? Citrate sounds like it could be deadly. Is this where I wanted to be ten years ago? Could I have been somewhere better by now? Why do I think right now is not good enough? Do I even want to be in a better place? Is this as good as my life will get, and I'm just not realizing how good it is? How do airbags come out so fast? How much of an effect is a decision I made five years ago having on my life right now? Should I have done this instead of that? Do herbal supplements do anything? I bet they're a total scam.

My mind is a complete mess. And to be honest, for my entire adult life, I don't think I've ever had any control over it. Not that anyone has complete control over their mind. What I'm talking about is the ability to think and decide for myself. During the last twenty-five years, it's almost as if I've been guided instead of living life how I want to. I feel like one of those kids on a leash at Disney World. There are so many fun things to do, but you can't do any of them because you're not in control. Someone else is. The fun is right there at your fingertips, but then you get dragged to the 'It's A Small World' ride. The older I became, the more I realized how little control I had, and the more I learned just how many mental illnesses I was suffering from. Luckily, a few of the disorders would taper off and not affect me so much. Obsessive-compulsive disorder and depression would creep into my life here and there and cause a ruckus. They would occasionally let it be known that they existed in the depths of my mind. They'd mess up my life for a week or so and then be gone.

Have fun with the destruction we caused. See ya!

Unfortunately, one mental disorder would stick around for good and turn my life upside down.

Driving is a haven for me. For some reason, moving down the freeway feels like an escape from whatever I am trying to escape from at that point in my life. If I am moving forward and leaving miles behind me, it feels like I am overcoming problems and obstacles in my life. I spend those miles wondering about many things. How the world works. Why are we here? What am I supposed to do while I'm here? And whatever that is, am I doing it right? On a scale of 1-10, how have I done so far in these forty-plus years? Is the direction I'm driving in right now the direction I'm supposed to be going at this exact time and point in my life? Should I have stayed and visited Mom longer? Should I have visited last weekend instead? The two-hour trips back and forth provided lots of time to think. And for someone in my condition, time is the enemy.

Bipolar mania. Bipolar depression. Obsessive-compulsive disorder. Severe Anxiety. Not a good combination. Now, try dealing with those things while also trying to answer the most important question of all.

What is my purpose?

I spend most of the time playing the license plate game wondering about my purpose. I performed a Google search of, 'What is the meaning of life?' That search provided over fourteen billion results. Let's put that into perspective. There are just over eight billion people on the planet. As a society, we are so curious about the reason for our existence that there are six billion more opinions about our existence than there are people living on the planet. To give you another perspective, a search of the word 'Christianity' yields only nine hundred and fourteen million results. Curiosity towards our existence is in our nature, like survival and love. Wanting to know why we exist is instilled in us. Unfortunately, it is *really* instilled in me. It is constantly on my mind. While we try to find every state license plate, I find myself in far-off wonderment. The open road can get you soul-searching for some reason. My problems. My rights. My mistakes. The whens, wheres, hows, and whys of life. Out of one hundred million sperm, why was I the one that had gotten through?

But before we try to answer all of that, let's go back to 2002, when the beginning of the rest of my life started, and the last bit of control I had was taken from me.

Tennessee

It's nine o'clock in the morning on a hot summer day in Fort Huachuca, Arizona. That's pronounced, wah-choo-kuh. Fort Huachuca is a smaller, quiet military post that sits halfway up a mountain just north of the Mexico/Arizona border and about forty-five minutes southeast of Tucson. If you have ever wanted to experience the worst weather on the planet then this is the perfect place for you. I remember thinking that it would make a great vacation spot for Satan. Instead of air conditioners, you have swamp coolers, which in the two years I was there I never really figured out how to properly operate. Instead of grass in your front yard, most people have rocks. Sounds just lovely, right?

On this particular day, our battalion commander is making a rare appearance at our Monday morning formation to inform us of an upcoming training exercise. He's attempting to motivate us with his usual 'if we don't get it right, no one else will' speech. Salutes are rendered and we are all sent to our smaller company formations for further instructions from our company commanders and platoon sergeants. My squad, along with three others, have made a semi-circle around Platoon Sergeant Thompson to obtain our duties for the day.

We know what we have to do for the day. It's the same as every Monday. But he sips from his coffee cup and barks the same instructions as if we have never heard them before. But wait, today's instructions include something new.

"Fill the vehicle fluids if needed. Inspect all tires. Log all deficiencies. Oh and by the way, before I forget, Sgt. Hughes will be conducting a class on underage drinking at 2300 hours this coming Friday night, and everyone must attend."

For those who don't know military time, 2300 hours is 11 p.m.

"Excuse me?", I said without hesitation.

"You heard what I said, Sgt. Hughes. Either you agree to conduct this class or you can go wait for me at the commander's office."

"I am not agreeing to something I know nothing about." My voice infused with a bit more attitude with each reply.

"The reason you are conducting this class is because two of your soldiers were arrested this past Friday night for public intoxication and underage drinking. The reason your class is at 2300 hours is becau…"

"If they're *my* soldiers and they were drinking underage on *Friday* then why have I not been informed until now?", I shouted.

"Do not interrupt me again, Sgt. Hughes! The reason

your class will be at 2300 hours is because that's when they were busted. You being their squad leader makes it your responsibility. Therefore you are giving a class on Friday night about underage drinking. Is that enough reason for you? And whatever your answer to that question is, it better conclude with 'Sgt. Thompson'. Is that clear?"

He had obviously sensed the attitude that I had included with my previous responses, and it seemed he felt the need to include some superiority in the rest of his parts of the conversation. I was game for the exchange that was about to take place. What he doesn't know is that at that point in my military career, superiority and respect for rank meant absolutely nothing to me anymore. The previous year I had been taken advantage of by my superiors. Let's just say I was tricked into taking the fall for something I didn't do. We'll just leave it at that. I'll give the details later.

"Do you agree to conduct the class, Sgt. Hughes?"

"Hell no! I am not giving a class about underage drinking due to two soldiers getting arrested when I hadn't even been informed that they were assigned to my squad. I haven't even met them!"

You read that correctly. I am being ordered to give a class because of the actions of two soldiers that I had never met. I didn't get the chance to give them any kind of guidance or paperwork on what's expected of soldiers in our unit. This drinking incident occurred three nights prior, yet no one called me to let me know they had been assigned to my squad when they arrived that Friday evening. No one called me later that same night when they were arrested. I immediately see what's about to happen, and it's not going to happen again. I'm being set up. Sgt. Thompson forgot to assign these two soldiers to a squad, and he knows it. His first instinct is to pass the blame on to me so his military record stays clean. It happens more than you would think. Good old military politics.

Sgt. Thompson doesn't realize it yet, but he has just become the fuel for what would be an unbelievable explosion of events over the next seven or so months. I say unbelievable because once you put everything together that you are about to read it's going to sound pretty unbelievable. But I assure you that the life events discussed herein actually occurred. Many family members and friends will attest on behalf of these events. Police, Military, and U.S. Marshal's records will prove it. I also use the word 'unbelievable' because it's supposed to add some kind of intrigue to the beginning of the story to keep you reading. Let me know if it worked.

"Excuse me, Sgt. Hughes?", he exclaimed.

"I didn't st-st-stutter. I will *not* conduct the cla…"

"At ease, Sgt. Hughes!"

Now, for those of you who aren't 'military', 'at ease' is a term that can be used in a few different ways. For instance, if an officer enters a room you are required to stand at attention, unless you are eating, and remain standing until he or she says 'at ease'. Meaning, thanks for recognizing my college degree, you may now be seated. 'At ease' is also used to put a formation of soldiers standing at attention into a more relaxed position while they are being given instructions.

Another way 'at ease' is used is to get a soldier who is acting out of line, well, back in line. When given this order in this way, you are to shut the hell up and prepare for an assault of vocabulary that will be broadcast within a few inches of your face at a decibel level that measures a bit louder than most dog barks. Now, 'at ease' is a position in which your legs are shoulder-width apart, your hands are intercrossed in the small of your back and your head and eyes are positioned straight forward to whomever is addressing you. On this day I did none of these things.

California

If you are unaware of military tactics and how respect towards military superiors works, let me give you a quick overview so that you may understand the severity of this particular situation. Wait, before we delve into that, I just want to point out that this entire book does not revolve around the military. This just happens to be where I chose to start because this is really when the mental disorders took over.

Moving on!

In 1996 I went to basic training at Fort Sill, OK. After a few days of in-processing and physical fitness tests, you are either declared fit for training or not fit for training. I was declared fit for training and I was damn proud of it. Or so I thought. It was about 1400 hrs, that's 2 p.m., and we were all relaxing in our barracks. That is until we heard a shout of authoritative instructions from outside that ranks up there with your mother using your middle name.

"Grab your gear and get on the truck! Now!"

I can guarantee you that I have never moved so fast in my entire life. Looking back at that moment I always laugh at the thought of all of us guys jumping up like we had just gotten caught masturbating. We were all immediately as scared as we could possibly be. We knew this moment was coming, we just had no idea when. One minute you're stopping to smell the roses. The next minute the roses are screaming in your face. We were frightened to our very core. But the fear soon vanished as we quickly focused our attention on grabbing our gear because none of us wanted to be the last person outside to meet the king-kong of a man who was waiting for us. Five minutes later we were all wearing our gear and standing shoulder to shoulder in a cattle truck. Yes, a cattle truck. If you're thinking of the aluminum trucks with holes all in them that you see on the freeway then you're thinking of the correct vehicle being used in this situation.

It was now time to step up and be as much of a soldier as we could be. We all had been found physically and mentally fit to be trained to protect the United States of America. We all volunteered. We were all proud and ready for what was to come during the next 9 weeks in the brutal summer of Oklahoma. But first, squats. We did squats with sixty pounds of full military gear on our backs while riding in a cattle truck from one side of the base to the other. What the hell did I just get myself into?

Ummm..hello? No one mentioned this when I signed up. This cattle truck ride was not in the brochure! Hello?

This was the beginning of being whittled down to the lowest

form of a human being possible so that the military could build us back up into the form and shape they wanted us to be in. It's kind of like a rebirth really. Everything you have and everything you have known is taken from you. And for the first few weeks of basic training, you are treated like, well, nothing.

The first thing that you learn when you get off of the cattle truck is how to shut the hell up. You then learn how to do push-ups. After that, you learn how to stand at attention, parade rest, and at ease. And next, you learn your place in the military, which is at the bottom. And the only way to get off of the bottom is to do what you are told every time you are told to do something and do it without question. Questioning a direct order in the military is like telling the judge in traffic court that yes you were speeding, no you're not paying the ticket, and yes you will speed again when you leave the courthouse parking lot.

You follow an order in the military and you respect your superiors whether you want to or not. You follow every order so that if you find yourself in battle it will be your instinct to immediately do what you are ordered to do for the success of the mission. Failure to follow an order may result in an Article 15, loss of rank and pay, a couple of weeks mowing and weed-eating the battalion offices every night, and prolonged embarrassment from everyone you work with. So now that we have the importance of following orders and respect towards your superiors covered, let's go back to that fateful Monday in Arizona.

On this particular morning, and for the first time in my military career, I did not shut the hell up. I did not cross my hands behind my back. However, I did prepare for an assault of explicit vocabulary, which was quickly met with an assault of my own. My actions on this day got me sent to the psychiatric ward at neighboring Ft. Bliss, TX. My time at this hospital was just the beginning of the absolute lowest point of my life. I would come face to face with my demon here, though not sure exactly what it was or how it would affect me, but our paths would cross for the first time at the Fort Bliss Psychiatric Ward. The demon had been within me for years, and it was ready to come out. It had been mistreated and ignored, and it wasn't happy. This was also the first of three psychiatric ward visits in the coming months. All three of which were at different institutions.

The look on everyone's faces when I refused my platoon sergeant's orders reminded me of the kids' reactions to the double-dog-dare in 'A Christmas Story'. As I explained earlier, in the military, you do what you are told, no matter if you agree or not. You just do it and you talk it out later. Up until this point in my six years in the military, I had always done what I was told to do and I did it without question. But this day would be the final day. This was the final time I was going to let someone put the fall on me instead of taking the blame themselves. It was the last time that I was going to cover up someone else's mistake just so their monthly evaluations remained clean. This was the last straw. And my demon was chewing on it.

Alabama

I don't think I have ever bragged about myself, at least not that I can remember. And since I haven't, let me take this opportunity to say that I do a great Brooks & Dunn impersonation. I've never boasted or put myself on a pedestal. But I will say that I pride myself on my military performance up until that day. I qualified as an expert on the M-16 and grenades while in basic training. I earned the Army Physical Fitness badge, which in itself is hard to do. You must score 270 or higher, with a minimum of 90 in all three categories of push-ups, sit-ups, and the 2-mile run. I also completed the Iron Man Challenge at Ft Sill, Oklahoma, and was a certified combat lifesaver. My monthly evaluations were pristine and I went above and beyond when performing my duties. So much to the point that I was promoted to corporal and assigned as a squad leader with ten soldiers working under me after just forty months of active service.

Corporal is a leadership position without the leadership pay. It is a common rank of pay in the Marines but a very rare rank in the Army. It is only given when a leadership position has been vacated and needs to be filled immediately. You are filling the role of a sergeant without yet going to sergeant's school. I was one of only three corporals in my PLDC class. The Primary Leadership and Development Course is the six-week course you must attend to become a sergeant. Accepting this leadership position without the leadership pay was a highlight in my military career and my life in general. My superiors had entrusted me to lead others without having been to leadership school. They saw my potential and hard work and rewarded me for it. Sadly, it was also the beginning of the end of my military career. Once I was in this position I was now the prime target for blame. And the blame came quickly.

Being ordered to conduct a class because of the actions of two soldiers I had never met was blame number two. What was the initial blame you ask? Well, two minutes after I was promoted to corporal I was assigned to be squad leader of the third squad of the first platoon. This squad included ten soldiers, three of whom were deployed at the time of my promotion. Along with the ten soldiers, this squad also came with millions of dollars worth of inventory and equipment. Equipment that a young corporal like myself didn't hesitate to sign for. About one-fourth of that equipment was lost overseas during deployment. Who would be given the blame for the loss of that equipment? This guy. Did this guy go on that deployment? No, this guy did not. I had been set up.

I was promoted and then assigned to a squad three days after it was determined that millions of dollars worth of equipment had been lost overseas. I would later find out during my inspection and inventory of the equipment that some items were moved and rotated so that I counted them twice, making it seem like all of the items were there. Once I saw that all of the inventory was "there", I signed for it. A few days later I was given an Article 15 for losing the equipment even though I wasn't even the squad leader at the time it was lost. Nice, huh? You'd be surprised what people will do to their own soldiers to speed up the advancement of their own rank and pay. Many promotions in the military are covered in blood.

Being blamed for these two occurrences wasn't the only reason I 'went off' as some people put it. A storm was brewing inside of my mind and had been for a long time. Years and years. The storm had gone forever unchecked, given no attention. Ignored my entire life. Three people fell victim to my out-of-control onslaught of disrespect that day. The first being my platoon sergeant, who quickly realized that he was in a no-win situation. The second was my platoon commander, Lieutenant Hilton. And third, my wife at the time, who had just married into the military and moved away from home for the first time in her life. There was no shouting or anything directed at her. But I'm sure dealing with what her husband had just done and having to be alone while he went off to a psych ward affected her in many ways. Sgt. Thompson had directed me to Lieutenant Hilton after his attempts to vocally restrain me had failed. Lt. Hilton was about to be put through a scenario that I'm sure was not covered during officer candidate school.

"First things first, Sgt. Hughes. You need to stand at attention when I speak to you."

My hands quickly went into my pockets, he knew then that

nothing he said from that point on was going to make any difference, but he tried anyway. At this point, the entire company was taking notice. Soldiers never put their hands in their pockets unless it was to retrieve something. You are taught this from Basic Training. Hands in the pockets NEVER.

"Sgt. Hughes! Do you have any idea the position you have put yourse...."

"Lt. Hilton! It would be in your best interest to get out of my face unless you would like that gold bar on your hat smashed through your forehead."

The silence after I threatened him had a Western movie feel to it. It would not have been weird at all if tumbleweeds had rolled by. I had just threatened a commissioned officer of the United States Army. My military career was now most likely over. With my hands still in my pockets I slowly turned and walked to my car. Not one person yelled at me to stop. I'm sure not one person wanted to try and make me. I got in the car and drove the 3-4 blocks to the military-issued home I shared with my wife. I got out and collapsed onto the doorstep between the driveway and the kitchen.

In the few minutes it took to make that drive, something had taken over my entire body and commanded me to give up on myself. And I did just that. I had reached the end. I had put so much effort into serving my country the best that I could, only for it to be torn apart by my superiors, and my mind. I was in a lose-lose situation. I was tired. I was mentally exhausted. I did not have a care in the world for what I had just done, but I was content with surrendering to the mental disorders that had restrained me for so many years. Every emotion I had been subconsciously holding in for so long was finally bursting out. Giving in and giving up seemed to provide a tremendous amount of comfort.

Louisiana

For a moment I actually felt at peace. And it was amazing while it lasted. Complete nirvana. I had never felt so relaxed in my life. So much weight was lifted. It was as if a valve had been opened up in my mind and tons of pressure was being released. That peace would be short-lived. I soon came to the realization that I had absolutely no control over what had just transpired. No control over my choices, my words, or my emotions. Nothing. Something forced me to disrespect my superiors. Something took away my ability to decipher the consequences of my words and actions. Something else had taken over and made its grand entrance. It rode in with a celebratory parade. It jumped out of a cake to fireworks in the background and the tune of AC/DC's 'Back In Black' as its intro music.

Here's Johnny!

The ride had begun and I had no way to get off. The restraint bar would not flip up. From zero to sixty in seconds.

My wife would soon find me sitting outside and within thirty minutes I was at the base hospital. Hours later I would end up at the psychiatric ward at Fort Bliss, TX. I can't recall exactly how much time I spent at Fort Bliss but I want to say around two months. After finally being properly diagnosed and medicated I was sent back to Fort Huachuca, AZ to await my discharge. I now had diagnosed mental disabilities and my service to my country was over and my record blemished. I had been torn away from the only thing I knew how to do. I devoted everything to my military career. It was my life. It was my purpose. I was doing it. I was living what I had thought to be my purpose. Some people go their entire lives without finding their true purpose and instead settle for whatever they can get out of life. I had been lucky enough to find my true calling, or so I thought. And before I could even blink it was all taken from me.

Now what is my reason?

The events that would unfold over the next 7 months would be the ultimate test of my existence on this Earth. I would pass this test but not without huge amounts of support from my family and those close to me. There were about to be many huge mistakes and failures. Some mistakes my bipolar disorder would make me think were the right things to do, no matter how obviously wrong they were. The little devil on my shoulder had a front-row seat to it all, and I was more than happy to let him enjoy every moment and do whatever he told me to do.

In the coming months, I would be discharged from the military. All I had to do was wait for my medical board evaluation, which takes months to conduct. Months of doing nothing was the last thing I needed given my mental state. My wife had already left to go back home due to her grandmother having some health problems. I was under the impression she was not coming back, and I don't blame her. I was now not the person she married. I wouldn't have come back if I were her. During this waiting period, I would hit an all-time low. I would be awake for days. I would wash my car every day. The outside one day, the inside the next day. I would spend all day turning the labels of the food in my cabinets so that they all faced forward. I would cry until I wasn't able to cry any longer and for no apparent reason. Probably due to the lack of control over everything. I would worry to the point my chest hurt.

No way was I going to continue this routine.

Once my time at the Fort Bliss Psych Ward was up I was reassigned to the Post Honor Guard back at Fort Huachuca. I was not allowed to work at an actual unit. No access to any weapons. I was useless to the military. And if I was useless to the military, I was useless on Earth. Realizing this is something that I cannot put into words. I had worked hard at this profession. I took pride in the patch on my arm. Pride in the fact that one day I may be running toward an enemy while others ran away from them. The military and the military way was my life. I was not a 'gung ho, let's go kill somebody' kind of soldier. But I made it a daily goal to excel at whatever that day presented to me.

Like Forrest Gump...I fit in the Army like one of them round pegs.

But now I no longer had a goal for each day. I no longer had a reason. Everything I knew was gone. Everything I prided myself in was gone. In an instant, I had no purpose. No worth. It is a terrible feeling. There could be thousands of people surrounding me and I would still feel alone. Lost.

I went active duty Army from the National Guard mostly to appease my father and to try and escape my parents' divorce. I most likely would have gone active duty anyway. Two weeks after I went active duty in the Army my father took his own life. Looking back I think I might have been the last family member to see him alive. He dropped me off at the hotel where I would stay until I was sent to Oklahoma for my first two years of active duty service. He didn't push me to serve, but he had mentioned and hinted at it a few times while growing up.

I had made it a point to do the best that I could do because the military was where he wanted me to be. I excelled at everything. Minimum was not in my vocabulary. I kept running when everyone else stopped. I trained when everyone else went home. Looking back I now see that the majority of everything I was doing was for him. It's as if the previous day wasn't good enough and I had to do better the next day. It was almost as if trying to be the best soldier in history was going to bring him back to life somehow. Or, was I trying to be the best soldier in history to distract myself from the fact that he had taken his own life? Was I intentionally occupying every minute of every day so I wouldn't have to think about not having a father? Looking back it seems like I was living for someone that had succumbed to mental disorders instead of living for myself. Now everything I had done to please my father's wishes was taken from me in an instant due to my mental disorders. I realize now that I had spent those previous years running from what he spent his whole life running from.

The discharge process from the Army had been taking its toll on me. I wasn't going to be able to handle much more time alone locked away in my own home. So what did I do? Or, what did me and the little devil on my shoulder do? We went to a local car dealership and told a salesman that I won the lottery but that I was waiting for my bank to approve the transfer. A few days later there was a white Pontiac Grand Prix in my driveway. A couple of weeks later I packed a bag, grabbed the dog, and hit the road. And the rest, as they say, is history.

With the military and Sierra Vista, AZ police in tow, I gave in to my current mental state and followed the directions of my mind. I had no control of myself or my decisions. I didn't know where I was going, but all roads would eventually lead me to myself. Did I even want to find my true self was the question.

Texas

In the coming weeks, which I'll go into more detail about later on, I would be introduced to what a manic episode is. I would travel from Arizona to Arkansas in the stolen Grand Prix. I would steal another car. I would steal stuff that would be pawned to pay for my expedition. I would steal money from my own grandfather. I would break into a family's home, ruin their entire Christmas, and steal all of their holiday memories from them. I would then make my way back to Monticello, AR where we used to live when I was young.

I would eventually make it all the way to Tunica, Mississippi where I spent a few days gambling my life away while several different law enforcement authorities were looking for me. I had also driven around and stolen Christmas cards from mailboxes hoping to find money. Stealing mail is a federal offense, so at that point, I had the U.S. Marshals on my tail. At the time, I had no idea who was looking for me or how close they were to finding me. I was not hiding at all. I was out in plain sight. Well, the demon was out in plain sight.

I was AWOL from the Army and had numerous felonies. Jail was inevitable. After a ten-day vacation from hell, I would eventually drive back to Jacksonville, AR, and turn myself in to my mother. She would be the driving force behind helping with all of the trouble I had gotten into. I owe my very existence to her. The book she had put together to prove that I wasn't a bad kid and to plead for a light sentencing was about three inches thick.

But I'm getting ahead of myself. That's all just an overview of what's to come. We'll get into the details of the car stealing and Tunica expedition later. It's early in the story and there's already been enough negativity. So let's go back in time and experience some happier, less troubling moments before we talk about 'the episode'.

Growing up I made my share of bad choices. Not anything worthy of jail time, but it had already been determined that I was going to be the child that caused trouble. Most families have that one child, right? I mean, I got my first ticket on the same day I got my license. Hello?! Troublemaker! I wasn't a constant bad child. I was more curious than anything. I wasn't a model child but I wasn't a hellish child either. I respected my parents and did what I was told, ….mmmmost of the time. I was more hard-headed than anything. Like most people, most of my bad decisions came in my teenage years. Prior to that, I was having too much fun on the farm in Monticello, AR to get into trouble. Ahhhh, the farm. Every time I think of it I can immediately smell the fields of tall grass that we spent our summers in. A game of hide and seek in a hay field could last all day, and we didn't mind.

You know how when you think back on your past there's that one memory or moment that always comes to mind? Well, for me that memory is fishing with my father. I've had many wonderful and happy moments in my life but my mind always goes back to fishing with him. And on the family farm in tiny Monticello, AR there was plenty of time for fishing. If you didn't fish or hunt you were considered weird. My brother Chris and I spent many days fishing and catching crawdads. Yes, 'crawdads' is the correct term. A piece of bologna tied to the inside of a milk crate and lowered into a creek always did the trick. Mom always got onto us for taking food from the fridge to feed to the creek critters. Nature and being outside was our way of life, that is until Mom or Dad turned on the back porch light signaling for us to start making our way across the fields and back home.

It doesn't get much better than growing up on a farm. There was always something to do and always trouble to get into. We slid down the roofs of barns. We had rock-skipping competitions. We rode four-wheelers until we ran out of all of the gas that we had stolen from everyone's houses on the farm. We climbed and played hide and seek in the haystacks of Uncle Harold's barn. Afternoons were spent eating persimmons on top of the tractor shed. We had to climb the shed to reach them so we just stayed up there. Triple dog dares to see who would eat the green persimmons were common. There were animals all over, endless woods and ponds to hike and discover. We would leave the house after breakfast and be gone all day. There were always things to do and always trouble to get into. A new experience with nature awaited each day. It was endless fun and the most enjoyable time of my childhood.

Missouri

Growing up I was mostly a happy child. For the most part, I usually kept to myself and was far from popular at school. I had a few friends but not many. I didn't go out of my way to meet new people. It just wasn't in my nature. I was happy playing alone if that's what I had to do. But being on the farm was great because there was always someone to play with. My brothers or my cousins were always around. You couldn't be alone if you tried to. There were four different houses on one farm, five if you included Pastor Qualls' home at the north end of the woods. Someone was always around. Weekend fish fry's behind the back pond were common. We'd chase lightning bugs and each other while the adults drank and talked about other adults who weren't there. Potato sack swings hung from the trees and chickens were clucking in the backyard.

We only spent a few years on the farm. We moved quite a few times across the state of Arkansas due to my parent's businesses. They opened some of the first EZ Marts in the state. My grandfather owned Pic N Pac in Jacksonville for many years and also owned other convenience stores. Owning and running a business was a family thing that was passed down to my father. It wasn't hard work but it was a lot of work and very time-consuming. Sometimes we'd get to spend the day at these stores. Sitting behind the cash register watching my parents work is where I was first introduced to adult magazines. When no one was looking I would take a quick peek behind the plastic card that covered the front picture. I was young and had no idea what I was looking at, but it was intriguing. I was a kid sitting at a gas station all day, what else was I supposed to do? Anyway, my parents were hard-working people. I can't remember a time when they weren't working. Dad worked during the day and mom had a factory job on the night shift. They supported the family well.

I'm not 100% sure but I think we moved to Monticello because of Dad getting a job with Terminix. He even had the giant bug on top of his truck. He would also go on to work for Pepsi and with Uncle Glen at the local hardware store. My grandfather then offered his convenience store to my parents. So after a few years in Monticello, we headed back to Jacksonville, AR, about twenty minutes northeast of Little Rock. I spent the majority of my teenage years in Jacksonville and Lonoke.

It wasn't a bad time in my life. I had friends from church and there were kids in the neighborhoods that I played with. But looking back I think these years are when I started to slowly build walls around myself. I had a difficult time determining my identity. I started acting out and doing stupid things to get attention. I missed the farm. I could be myself on the farm and do whatever I wanted. Now I was growing up and I had to start doing more mature things and make mature choices, something I did not take too kindly to. Besides basketball and fishing, I don't recall many things in my teenage years that ever really excited me or made me happy. I had a few girlfriends but I had no idea how to be a boyfriend. If any past girlfriends are reading this I truly apologize. It's not that I didn't care about you, it's that I didn't care about relationships in general. I would much rather have been on a basketball court or in a fishing boat than getting all foofy smoochie with a girl.

But the deeper I got into my teenage years the more distant I became to everyone. It was hard for me to find anything that made me happy. That's why when I knew a fishing trip was coming up I always said yes. My older brother Chris often went but it was usually me and Dad. Little brother Robert was too, well, little. Fishing got me away from everything. It was an escape from…whatever I was escaping from. It was time spent with a man that wasn't around much, but a man that made it a point to do something with us now and then. He was busy, we knew this. So when the opportunity came to sit in total silence on a lake with my dad I never turned it down.

He was a quiet man. A small man. Short, and skinny like most in his mother's family. But what he lacked in size he made up for with his work ethic. He ran many small businesses and ran them well. Because of this, we didn't see much of him. He usually got home at dinner time and spent most nights adding up the sales from that day. He was not the type to show affection nor was he the type to show hate or anger. I can't remember a single time in my life where he got into an argument with anyone, about anything. He would bark the occasional "well shit" while working on something but that was it as far as language went. You never heard him curse or even raise his voice much.

I also can't remember a single time when he told me he loved me. Not once. I do not hold that against him. He was not raised in an affectionate household. I knew he loved me and that he cared for all of us. He showed his affection and appreciation in other ways. One of those ways was by taking us fishing. Looking back now on all of those fishing trips it seems he was using them to try and escape things as well. Most people go fishing to escape the daily grind and the fast pace of life. My father was escaping from demons. He was escaping from himself. Many years later I would find myself doing the exact same thing.

One fishing trip in particular is carved deep into my mind. As I mentioned before, Dad very rarely cursed. But on this particular trip, I would learn many words that I shouldn't have, some of which I'm sure he had made up on his own. A sailor would have no chance against the epic onslaught of curse words that came from his mouth on this particular day. It would be the first time in my life I would witness anger from my father. The anger was not directed at me. I took comfort in knowing that I did nothing to provoke this onslaught of adult-rated vocabulary. I also took comfort in knowing that I had new words to share with my buddies at school.

So who was he taking this anger out on? No one. He was mad at the windshield wipers that weren't working. Spending all day on a lake catching nothing followed by a drive home in the rain with no windshield wipers is not a good combination.

My father was beyond mad. There was more than frustration coming from him. He was mad at the windshield wipers, yes, but he was letting it be known that he was upset about other things. Years and years of anger and depression were billowing out of him. He snapped. Witnessing this anger from my father was beyond scary because I had never seen him act that way before. Looking back on that day, what was even more scary was how quickly he changed back to normal.

Mississippi

There are moments in life that rattle you to your core. Moments that you spend countless hours trying to understand only to never quite grasp what exactly happened or why it happened. There have only been three instances in my life where I have been legitimately scared.

1. Witnessing The Gurdon Light in Gurdon, AR,(I ran and screamed).

2. Receiving my transfer papers to serve a year in Korea.

3. This particular fishing trip.

I have shared this story before, but I've always left out the part about my dad practically transforming into…well, I don't really know what he transformed into, but it was not human.

This fishing trip started out like all of the others. But it wouldn't end like all of the others. Knowing that I was going fishing with my dad the next morning usually meant no sleep that night. I was always excited. Like a child on Christmas

Eve, there was no way I was going to go to sleep. But my eyes would get heavy at around midnight, so I usually got a few hours of sleep before Dad would wake me up around 5 a.m. The car was usually already loaded the night before, so all we had to do was get up, get dressed, and go. Me in my usual shorts that used to be pants, and dad in his puffy vest that he got from some company he used to work for and a mesh baseball cap from another company he used to work for. Most of our coolers and such had cigarette and other brand labels on them. We got a lot of free stuff through the companies we sold products for at our stores. It's funny how you can remember such small details like that. Anyway, breakfast was usually a honey bun and chocolate milk grabbed from our own gas station.

I was never a morning person, so staying awake was hard for me, even with all of the excitement of catching tons of fish. I was usually already dozing off while Dad was fueling the car and getting coffee. The sound of a slamming door on an 80's era Oldsmobile will usually wake you up pretty good though. I would perk up when Dad got back in and cranked up the tank. We called it the tank because, well, it was a tank. It was a giant of a car. It was so big it sometimes felt like all of the other cars were swerving off of the road to avoid us. I felt so small riding in that thing. Faded yellow with black vinyl interior didn't exactly scream 'check out my ride' either. But what it lacked in appearance it made up for with dependability. Mmmost of the time.

It was now about 5:30 in the morning and the trip to Lake Conway had begun. Our store was on the northern end of

Jacksonville, so we would take the back way to Lake Conway, West on Highway 89. Dad didn't talk much. The rides were usually quiet. He was focused on driving and not smoking the cigarette that he would put in his mouth as soon as we were out of Mom's sight. The weird thing is that he never lit it. Many times I saw my dad with a cigarette in his mouth. Not once did I see him actually smoking one. Whatever works I guess. Glancing over at my father I saw a determined man guiding our tank into battle, preparing for the onslaught of fish that were going to be jumping into our boat. They didn't stand a chance. The closer we got to the lake the bigger our eyes became.

When driving the back way to Lake Conway you can see glimpses of the lake through the trees before you get to the lake itself. While Dad cruised along the winding back roads listening to CCR, I would pick out the best fishing spots as we got closer and closer. After about thirty-five minutes we had arrived, not at the lake, but at the snack shop. Dad always loaded up on Vienna Sausages and crackers and I usually filled my pockets with Slim Jims. Add a few Cokes and water bottles into the Marlboro cooler and we were off to the docks.

Dad always went to the same dock every trip. He would make his way into the bait shop to talk with the guys about who caught the biggest what and where while I unloaded the car. I didn't mind. It wasn't much to unload. Plus it kept me from having to pretend to laugh at the old guys' fishing jokes inside the bait shop. Dad would pay for a boat and motor rental, life jackets that were used as seat cushions, another coffee and we would be on our way. Some of my fondest moments with my father are of us standing on the dock in complete silence right before we got into the boat, the sun trying to wake up, and birds already in song. After a brief moment, he would pat me on the shoulder, his loving way of saying 'Finish loading the boat and let's go.'

Lake Conway is a beautiful lake with many Cypress trees rising up to the skies. It's not one of the better lakes in Arkansas for fishing though. You could occasionally fill an ice chest but most trips weren't worth bragging about. After about an hour you kind of already knew how the rest of the day was going to be. Dad breaking out his sausages usually meant his excitement had dwindled and he was now in 'I don't care' mode. We hadn't caught a thing. Not even a nibble. Many coves and bridges had been fished without any luck. We soon came to the realization that we would be going home with nothing. We didn't mind. We both enjoyed each other's company, even if we never admitted it. Both of us had escaped whatever it was we were running from. We were at peace on the lake.

At the time, I had no idea of the lack of control my father had over his mind. Years later I would learn about his many thoughts of suicide. When you're a kid no one tells you of such things. You have no idea. You assume the man that's sitting across from you in the boat is perfect. He helped raise you. He feeds you. He clothes you. He keeps you in line. According to you, he can do no wrong and he is in control of all situations.

The comfortable silences were usually interrupted by me casting my line into a tree. Dad would have to reel in his line, click on the trolling motor, spin the boat around, and halfway climb a tree to untie my line while halfway standing on the end of the boat. I caught many trees. Very rarely did he show frustration when he had to untangle me.

"You want me to just cut the line?", I would ask.

"No! Don't cut it.", he always replied.

Dad was smart. He knew that cutting the line and restringing my Zebco would take twice as long as him untangling it from a tree would, no matter how dangerous it was.

"If I fall in throw me one of those seat cushions."

After about five hours of only catching trees, Dad decided it was time to head back to the docks. He would put another cigarette in his mouth that would never get lit then start up the two-horsepower trolling motor and aim the boat for the cove we came from. Going back to the dock with an empty cooler is not what anyone looks forward to. No fish usually meant a quick dock and car load and gettin' gone. This way we wouldn't have to explain our terrible fishing performance to the bait shop owner. Just get in the car and go. We timed it just right. After getting in the car the clouds slowly started to form. A good old Arkansas thunderstorm was rumbling its way towards us. A day of catching nothing followed by a rainy trip home. Awesome.

Oregon

We were about fifteen minutes into the ride back home when the sprinkles started making music on the windshield. Dad casually reached behind the steering wheel and clicked on the wipers. To his surprise, nothing happened. He clicked them again. Nothing. He removed the unlit cigarette from his mouth and I knew then that things were about to get serious. He turned off the radio, I assumed so he could think more clearly. After fiddling with the wiper switch for a couple more minutes he eventually gave up since he could no longer see through the windshield. He pulled the tank over to the side of the road and got out to do his best mechanic impersonation. At this point, it is pouring down rain and my father is standing by the car getting soaked while staring at wipers that don't want to work.

"Turn on the wipers when I say!", he shouted.

I jumped over to his seat and searched for the switch. Dad grabbed the wipers with his hands and moved them across the windshield.

"Now!"

I hit the switch. Nothing. After doing this many times he gave up and made his way back into the car. Now I've heard cursing before, either at school or on the basketball court. But as he opened the door to get back in the car I heard the most obscene and vulgar words I had ever heard slowly getting louder and louder the wider the door opened. I had only ever heard my dad curse when the Razorbacks gave up a touchdown or while he was trying to fix something. But this wasn't cursing. This was downright spewing of R-rated vulgarity that deserved some kind of Guinness World Record. Mature content. Not suitable for children. Words that would bring a frat party to a screeching halt. Ten minutes ago my dad had exited the car to look at the wipers, something else got back in. I don't know who or what it was but it wasn't my father. Once seated back in the car he gave the steering wheel a left hook. The dashboard received multiple uppercuts and the center console took a few good body shots from the tiny man that had seemingly reached his end. It looked like he was on the verge of crying out, but it seemed as if he was struggling to do so. He wanted to, he just wasn't capable. It's almost as if he wasn't allowed to.

I was frozen. I mean, what do you do when you've just witnessed your father in a heavyweight title bout with an Oldsmobile? I had never seen my father act in such a way in all my life. He never whipped us as kids, Mom would not allow it. I don't think he ever wanted to anyway. The worst thing my father ever did to me was smack me on the back of the head when I got that ticket the same day I got my license. He and my mother were on the front porch when I walked up and told them. They immediately grounded me and sent me to my room. He opened the door for me and walloped me across the back of the head as I passed. But that was it. That was the only time I can remember him ever putting a hand on me. He just wasn't a physical person at all. So to see him act in this way was very surprising. And very scary.

He was soaked from head to toe. The vinyl seats absorbed none of the water. So he just sat there in a puddle the whole way home. Water splashed throughout the car as he removed clothing and thrashed his head back and forth while spewing curse words that hadn't even been made up yet. Knowing what I know now, looking back it seems he was trying to release whatever was in control of him. He wasn't mad at the windshield wipers. He wasn't mad at the rain. He wasn't mad at not catching a single fish. He was mad at his mind. Mad at his inability to control his thoughts and emotions. He was mad because he went fishing to escape reality and ended up running into more of it. He had been depressed and struggled with mental disorders for years. Majority of his life even. He had kept it all inside. It was all coming out, just like it came out of me that day in Arizona. And I just happened to be the one to witness it happening. Not a single word was projected at me. It was almost as if I wasn't even there. And it was almost as if he wasn't there. Dad stepped out of the car. A demon stepped back in.

This onslaught of anger lasted about five minutes and then his demeanor instantly changed back to a confusing calmness. One minute the devil was ripping his body in half and escaping from his torso. The next minute he was relaxed and leaning back in his seat, putting a cigarette in his mouth that he would never light. We sat in silence for a few minutes. I was too terrified to say anything. He seemed to have released whatever he had been holding in and was content in sitting there until the storms subsided. They never did.

He found a car wash and pulled under the awning to get out of the rain. He did more mechanic stuff and eventually found the problem. A blown fuse. Did we have an extra fuse that particular size? No, we did not. For the remaining fifteen minutes of the trip, my father drove 15 mph through pouring rain while pushing the wipers across the windshield with a rod he found near the car wash and then pulling them back again with a string. Rod, string, rod, string. This man just spent his day off getting up at 5 a.m. to drive thirty-five minutes to catch nothing and then drove another thirty-five minutes back home in the rain with no wipers.

I remember feeling so small and helpless in that front seat while looking over at my father as he reached out to move the wipers again and again. I wanted so badly to help, but there was just nothing I could do. He put on a clinic and worked with what he had. He persevered. He was determined. I was scared. He was getting us home, no matter what it took. With an unlit cigarette hanging out of his mouth and a determined yet disgusted look on his face, he reminded me of a general leading our tank into battle.

"Bring up the left flank damn it! Hold the line!"

I knew he wouldn't falter in this mission. He got us home

safely and he and I never spoke of that fishing trip ever again.

43

North Carolina

Up until that day I had considered my father to be happy with his life. No one told me otherwise. Parents don't tell their kids that kind of stuff. He seemed to enjoy running a business. He seemed content with where he was at. Deep down he was not. I had no clue anything was wrong with him until I witnessed everything flowing out of him in a terrifying rage. I didn't know what it was, but I knew it wasn't natural. No one should get that angry at windshield wipers. I knew something was not right with him, but I was young and didn't know about depression and mental illnesses. I knew he was mad, I also knew he was mad at other things besides windshield wipers, I just had no clue what it was.

He had been holding things in for years. Recently, while writing this book, I would learn that he planned his suicide numerous times. He didn't just think about suicide, he planned it. He had been unhappy and extremely depressed for a long time, and he just wanted someone to know. Even if that person was his teenage son who could do absolutely nothing about it. He just wanted it all out of him. He wanted control. Control of his mind. Control of his emotions. Control of the ability to choose to be happy or even be sad. As scared as it made me at that moment, I've always hoped he released whatever it was that he was trying to remove from his soul, and from his mind.

Now imagine for a moment that you have such a terrible illness that you actually plan out your suicide on numerous occasions. Take a moment and think about how many wires have to be crossed to be okay with thinking about how you are going to leave this earth. You've been given the ultimate gift of being able to roam this planet for as long as you possibly can. Yet your disorder doesn't allow you to see how your gift turns out. This man went about his daily life like everyone else. But while he's sitting and watching TV with you, he's thinking about how he's going to end his existence while you're thinking about the trouble that Steve Urkel just got into. He went to church. He went to work. He sat on the porch and tried to enjoy the day just like you do. He did everything you and I do. But inside he was slowly dying. In his mind, he had already been dead for many years. He had lost control of everything long ago. Life at this point was simply him doing what his disorders told him to do.

Be sad. Be depressed. Don't enjoy that! Make this decision, not that one. Do what I say!

Every time we would drive past a cemetery he would always point and make the 'people are just dying to get in there' joke. Now looking back it must have been so hard for him to make that joke, knowing that a part of him wanted to be in that very cemetery. It was as if he was driving past where he thought he belonged. Some people belong in the military. Some people belong in a doctor's office. Some belong in a school teaching. My dad felt he belonged in a cemetery. It's where he wanted to be. That is such a sad thought. I'm crying right now. Not because he's gone, but because of how lost and painful things must have been for him, for anyone to feel that way. He hid it all very well, at least from us kids he did. But you can't hide the demon forever. It eventually gives away its hiding place. Something I would find out on my own.

Inside he was unhappy. Inside he didn't want any part of life on Earth. He was so enslaved by demons inside of him that he would rather not exist than spend endless days *trying* to enjoy life. When you are tied down by these mental chains you spend every minute of your existence *trying*. The enjoyment doesn't come naturally. You have to work for it, and the work is extremely tiring. It's exhausting. And it lasts for days, months, years even, until you conclude that you'll never be able to be naturally happy. You will spend the rest of your days forcing yourself to be happy. Trying to be happy. Begging to be happy. Unless you get help of course. We'll get into getting help later on.

You can be happy again. Please know this. It is possible to find yourself again. To find your happiness again. Happiness is and always will be inside you. It hasn't been taken and removed from your body. It's been covered up and smothered. The feelings can be reversed. It's not going to happen overnight. And it will require work on your part. But please know that if you are depressed and feel overwhelmed by things out of your control, you can be happy again. You can have control of your life again. I beg you to please know this.

Unfortunately, in my father's mind, he probably figured that he wasn't going to be able to do so. But he never sought constant help or treatment, something that would have probably saved his life. He had battled for many, many years, decades even. He probably assumed that the thoughts in his mind would get worse and worse to the point that not living was better than living like he was. He did not seek the long-term care he needed to overcome these things. Which is what you will need to do if you want to take charge of your life and your disorders. Eventually, he would end up at the Bridgeway Mental Health facility, a last-ditch effort to try and stop what he probably already knew was going to happen. In early January of 1998, he would drop me off at the Army enlistment center for me to begin my active duty service in the Army. This would be the last time I see my father.

Two weeks later…

"Private Hughes! Where's Private Hughes?"

I was in the back of a truck in full gear. Our platoon was just about to pull out and go on a training exercise with the rest of our unit.

"Over here, Sergeant!", I yelled from the back of the truck.

"Private, you need to report to the First Sergeant's office. Immediately."

I looked around the truck and made eye contact with everyone there. I had done nothing wrong, so I knew that whatever was happening was serious. Hell I had only been there for two weeks, I hadn't been in the Army long enough to do anything wrong, and everyone else in the truck knew that. Everyone's expressions changed very quickly after hearing the order to go see the First Sergeant. I ran about a block from the motor pool to our battery office building with the most confused and worried look on my face. I went inside the lobby and stopped to catch my breath and removed all of my gear. A few people passed by with 'already knowing' looks on their faces, which made me even more worried.

I made my way down the hall, forced myself to knock on the First Sergeant's office door, and waited for permission to enter.

"Come!"

I closed the door and centered myself on his desk. "Private Hughes reporting as ordered, First Sergeant."

"At ease, Private."

He took a long, deep breath, then looked down at his desk, then slowly raised his eyes to meet mine. What I saw was not good. The eyes never lie. He struggled to get out his next words.

"Private Hughes…. You are to go into the office across the hall and pick up line two. Now… I want you to take as much time as you need. Understood?"

"Yes, First Sergeant."

I snapped to attention and left his office. The hallway was six feet wide. It felt like twenty. I closed the door and turned around to see the line two light flashing, almost as if to say 'warning', 'warning', every time it blinked.

I took a deep breath… and another.

I stood there shaking, staring at the blinking light. My heart rate increasing with each red flash of emergent illumination. The last thing I wanted to do was push that button. I wanted time to stop. I knew that whatever I was about to find out was not going to be good. My family already knew. My military superiors already knew. I was about to know.

'Click'

"Hello? Is this Private Jeremy Hughes?"

"Yes?"

"This is the Red Cross. Private Hughes, please state your social security number for verification."

"###-##-####."

"Thank you. Please hold while I transfer you."

"Jeremy?"

"Yes?"

"This is Teresa..........it's Dad."

Kansas

Time immediately came to a standstill. Everything around me ceased to exist. I don't remember anything else my sister may have said or even me replying to her. All I remember is complete silence. I might have even hung up on her, I'm not quite sure. What I do remember is being huddled over a toilet and throwing up. Anything that happened between finding out and being bent over the toilet is a blur to me. It was a shock to my system. And it only got worse as the weeks went by. Like when it finally hit me that I couldn't pick up the phone and call him anymore. He was no longer there at the push of a few buttons.

Death, it's something that I am terrified of. I currently suffer from severe anxiety and panic attacks. My heart rate climbs to about 140 and my blood pressure shoots up instantly and death is an immediate thought every time these attacks happen. Not being on this planet in a living, physical form is emotionally excruciating to me. I hate that it's a part of my life. A life that is way too short. If we were able to live thirty to forty years longer then it probably wouldn't bother me as much. One of the things that irks me so much about life is that the last thirty or so years of it you aren't even able to do what you used to. The second half of your life is spent recovering from what you did in the first half, and the last 1/4 of your life is usually spent in a wheelchair or a bed or nursing home. Well, that sucks! By the time you get over the hill and start down it, your active years are pretty much over and the rest of your life is spent in recovery mode, for most people anyway. There are a handful of people who are active in their sixties and up, but very few.

I started getting gray hair in my beard at age twenty-seven, right after my first son was born. I just spelled 'son', 's-u-n'. I had to go back and correct it. Lord, help me. Anyway, the physical appearances of old age like gray hair hit me early, so maybe that kickstarted my fear of growing old and death. I mention all of this to say that we know death is coming. We don't know how, when, where, why, and nothing can ever prepare us for it. Even though we wake up every day knowing it may be our last, we are never prepared for it.

Maybe it's not that I'm so scared of death. Maybe it's feeling as if all of my time was wasted because I was so constricted by mental disabilities, that I wasn't able to fully enjoy my life because of them. It's as if I was put here only to be tested every single day, then find my calling and purpose in the military only to have it ripped away from me. Why even put me here at all if that's the case? Why am I so scared of dying? Is it because of the fear of looking like a failure in the Lord's eyes? Where will I go when I die?

I stole cars. I stole money. I ran from the police. I broke into a home. I went AWOL from the military. I did those things because mental disorders overtook my life and my mind. Do I go to hell for doing those things? Well of course I'm scared of going to hell. Who wouldn't be? From what I hear it's no spa treatment. I don't think it's mostly death that I'm scared of. I think it's not determining my purpose before I leave this Earth. Did my father figure out his purpose? Was not finding his purpose a reason he took his own life? Was it his inability to not be able to find his purpose because of mental disorders that made him resort to suicide? Was he addicted to finding his purpose like I am?

The second funeral I remember attending was for my brother Ben, my dad's son from his first marriage. Benjamin Hardy Hughes took his own life on July 18th, 1993 at the age of twenty-four. He had recently gone through a divorce. He was found in his truck in the middle of a field with a self-inflicted gunshot wound. Our father, Virgil Hardy Hughes Jr, took his own life on Jan 28th, 1998 at the age of fifty-two. He had recently gone through a divorce and had battled depression for decades. He was found inside his car at a rest area at the Greers Ferry Lake Dam in Heber Springs, Arkansas with a hose attached to the exhaust and run through the trunk.

From chapter six you already knew my father had taken his own life. But nothing prepared you for what you just read, did it? See what I mean? Death is there. It's everywhere. All around us. We hear about it every day. Approximately 1.8 people die per second. Almost five people will die in the time it takes you to read this sentence. It happens so often it's an afterthought for most. No matter how much we know about it. No matter how much we try to prevent it. No matter how much we try to ignore it. It's there. I just happen to be one of the people that can't ignore it. My eyes water when I read news stories regarding death. Even the deaths of animals in the nature documentaries that I watch make me sad. This huge lion is chowing down on the neck of a gazelle having the meal of its life. And I'm sitting on the couch fighting back watery eyes hoping the gazelle had a great life up until that point.

If we as a society can so easily ignore death then of course mental disorders are being ignored dramatically.

The quote 'circle of life', to me, is just colorful wrapping paper on a casket. It's just another way to make death not seem so bad. I wish I didn't dread it. I wish I could ignore it and enjoy each moment and just deal with death when I get older. I just can't do that. Why? Because I have things going on inside my brain that prevent me from being able to do that. And I always will. *You* might have the ability to ignore death because *your* brain is wired to be able to do so. I think about death daily because my brain is wired to do so. I do not choose to think about death as often as I do. I do not choose to have severe panic attacks. I do not choose to be bipolar. I do not choose to have OCD. It's how I am wired, and it's a hard life.

My father was the first person I saw dead. I was nineteen. Seeing my father in a casket is something I have yet to be able to put into words. The day I found out he died my first sergeant made me stay the night at his home, a sign of compassion that I hold dear to this day. He didn't even ask me if I wanted to. He just told me to go upstairs from his office to my barracks room and pack a bag.

"You're coming home with me tonight, Private."

I went active duty in the Army in early January of 1998. A few weeks later, after the memorial service, I was peeking around a corner in the funeral home watching my sister Teresa place mementos inside our father's casket. There he was, lying peacefully. The last time I saw my father so relaxed was years prior in the middle of Lake Conway on one of our fishing trips. He finally found his forever peace. His demons were gone. His depression was gone. His pain was gone. His struggle to be naturally happy was gone. But he was gone.

He looked so comfortable. I'm glad I got to see him one last time. I'm even more glad that he looked so free of mental distress. Now knowing how much he struggled with mental disorders, and seeing how peaceful he was, it now makes sense. Back then at nineteen years old, it made no sense at all. But now, knowing what he went through his entire life, and what I have gone through my entire life, I understand, somewhat. He sought the Lord his entire life. He may never have found his purpose, but he had faith in where he was going to end up. He had succumbed to terrible disabilities that he fought his entire life, but he found his peace. I am under the impression that he was partly okay with leaving this Earth because he knew where he was going to end up, and that ending made him happy, which was probably the only natural happiness he had experienced in a very long time. I don't think he ever actually wanted to go through with it. But if that was the only happiness the disorder was offering, he was in no mental shape to decide otherwise.

Some say that suicide is selfish. That people that commit suicide have no idea what it does to those they leave behind. That it's the easy way out. Let me tell you something, fighting depression for decades is not 'easy'. These critics only look at the end result. They overlook the fact that that person may have been putting up a good fight for many years, which is not 'easy'. In my opinion, people contemplating suicide can't acknowledge those things or feel those emotions. These disorders have complete control. The people suffering can't think of others during that moment because they don't have the ability to. They have no control over what is happening. If a person has gotten to the point where suicide is an option, then they are no longer able to consider how their actions will affect others.

Proclaiming that a person who has no control over what is happening is selfish is simply asinine. They aren't being selfish. They aren't giving up. They're considering suicide because their disorder has offered it as an option to escape from what the disorder has been putting them through. Many fight back, and for long periods of time, until they can't any longer. Many also fight back and overcome these situations. It happens all the time. People overcome mental hardships every single day. Some, however, are so overcome that instant relief is needed.

My father made it fifty-two years, and did it battling mental disease for the majority of that time. I will forever believe that he put up a good fight. Before my father's death, he had gotten a new job and was living with my sister until he could get his own place. My sister lived in Maumelle, AR. Greer's Ferry Dam, where my father took his own life, is sixty-four miles from Maumelle. Approximately a one hour and fifteen-minute drive north up Highway 5. Now, to those who say that suicide is the 'easy way out', how easy do you think that sixty-four-mile drive was for my father? Do you see him voluntarily pressing the gas and turning the wheels of that car for every mile, getting closer and closer to death? I don't. He wasn't driving that car. Just like I wasn't driving the car when I was on the run.

The vines of his disorder that were intertwined throughout his brain were driving that car. He had been battling and seeking out happiness for decades. All he saw was an escape. Fortunately, for most people, we never see our deaths coming. He faced his death for *sixty-four miles*. An hour and fifteen minutes. If you think there is anything easy about that please feel free to explain. Knowing that his life was about to end had to be gut-wrenching. I imagine him crying that entire drive. Sixty-four miles of sorrow, mental agony, and indescribable pain. But he knew he was about to be free of everything. Eventually, to him, that freedom was worth the trip. All he saw was relief from it all. He could not see anything beyond that. He didn't have the ability to calculate, comprehend, or change his decision.

If you know someone who would consider his one hour and fifteen-minute drive to death as an 'easy way out', please share this story with them.

Oklahoma

In no way do I condone suicide. Personally, I believe none of us want to die and that anyone who takes their own life had some kind of disorder that they were struggling with. Sure there are rare instances of taking one's life after committing murder or various other serious crimes. Or even taking your life in jail due to a guilty conscience or to avoid lifetime confinement. Even in those cases, I believe there is some kind of mental disorder contributing to the decision to end one's life. But it's human nature to survive at all costs. To fight and live on and to will your way towards another day. To be so enthralled by a disorder to *want* to die and leave this earth is so mind-boggling and confusing to me.

There are so many trials and battles that come along with mental disorders. Let's face it, reprogramming the brain, the most complex thing in the world, is not possible. Retraining the brain is, but rewiring and reprogramming the brain to not have a mental issue is just not possible. Not that I know of anyway. It's not just the disorder you fight. What you also end up fighting is the stigma. Name-calling. People's opinions. Side effects of medications. And the worst one of all, for me anyway, accepting the fact that you have a mental illness. Accepting the idea that you have a problem. That you aren't perfect. That you have a weakness. That you're different. Society, for the most part, doesn't accept 'different'. Society searches for and points out 'different'. Society embarrasses and makes fun of 'different'. So not only is accepting the disorder hard, but knowing that others know you have a disorder is also hard.

In my opinion, a mental illness is an illness forever. You cannot get rid of it. You can maintain it and somewhat put it on the back burner, but the root cause will always be there, especially for severe cases. And knowing that it's always there is also another issue you have to deal with. It's one thing to be depressed. It's another to be depressed and know you'll probably be fighting that depression for the rest of your life. Now it is possible to overcome depression about certain things. Let's say you moved away to go to college and you've never been away from home before and you fall into a depressive state. That can be a tough time for any young adult. But that's fixable.

I'm talking about serious stuff here. Not that being depressed about moving away from home isn't serious, because it is. All forms of mental complications are serious. However, clinical depression has recurrences and can last for a very long time. Imagine battling sadness for years. Now imagine battling sadness for years, and during that time you're on and off numerous medications trying to find one that works. And each medication you try has its own side effects, some of which can make your mental problems worse. Now imagine battling all of that and also dealing with how those around you look at and think of you.

You get so used to covering up what you're going through that the cover becomes comfortable. So comfortable that you use that cover even when you're alone. The cover could be a blanket of thorns, but you welcome it if the pain from the thorns isn't as bad as the pain from the illness. You lock up your fight against the disorders. You throw away the key. Not realizing that each day you ignore it only multiplies its power. Ignoring your disability is comfortable. It's easier. You aren't wasting energy battling it. The daily grind is hard enough. Then you have to exert even more energy trying to deal with whatever is wrong with you. It's tiring. It's draining. It's weakening. You become so tired and weak from battling it all that you just cover it up and pretend it isn't there. The exhaustion you feel seems to make what you're going through even worse. It gets to the point where you no longer want to face it, simply because you no longer have the mental or physical strength to face it. You've put forth every ounce of your being just to be happy for one second, only to sit in emotional darkness and watch each second of your life tick away.

I refuse to acknowledge that I have mental problems! I am Superman! I am healthy!

If you haven't noticed by now, I tend to skip around and just type and blurt out whatever comes to my mind while my fingers are on the keyboard. At that moment it makes sense to me. Hopefully. But I told myself when I started writing this that I would be real, honest, and true. I would write what I felt and what my mind wanted to write. I'm sure my disorders are writing some of this for me and I'm okay with that. I'm not writing with Nobel Prize intentions. I'm simply writing something to share among others who may also suffer, and even those who don't.

Moving on!

I do not have disorders! I am not mentally weak! I am fine! Just let me be fine! I refuse to take these medications. Nope. Not happening!

Each pill alarm on my phone is a reminder of my disabilities.

'Hey, you. Bipolar guy. It's 10:00 p.m. Just reminding you that you have mental problems! It's time for you to take those pills that make you somewhat normal because you can't do it on your own!'

That's what it feels like. Every pill that you take every day is a reminder. A reminder that you are different. A reminder that something in your brain isn't right. That's a hard pill to swallow every single day and night. Another thing that is hard to accept in the fight to get control of your disorder is how long it takes to see any improvement. Your doctor tells you to take so many pills so many times a day. You'll be fine, in 4-6 weeks. Six weeks? That's comforting. How much do I owe you for such encouraging words, Doc? What do I do until then? Just remain miserable?

Disorders are hard. And those without them only see the

ONE thing you have, whether it be depression, bipolar, or any other illness. They don't see everything else that goes along with it that I've just listed. Out of everything, the disorders themselves, the stigma, the time it takes to get better, and the medication searching, the one thing that slowed down my improvement the most was refusing to accept the fact that I had a mental disorder. On many occasions, this refusal led to me ending my medication treatment and spiraling into a depressive or manic phase. I had been in a few of these manic episodes before I was diagnosed with anything, I just didn't know what it was or what I was going through at the time. I just thought me staying up for days on end and being a huge neat freak was normal.

But over time the disorders you're born with get worse and things happen in your life that add to those disorders. Your brother takes his own life when you're fifteen. Your parents get divorced when you're 18. Your father takes his own life. You leave home for years to be all you can be in the Army until one day you discover that you'll never be all you can be.

You'll be whatever your mental illnesses allow you to be.

Florida

Now that you have an idea of the mental hardships within my family's history, let's go back to that day in Arizona, when my Army career came to an abrupt end, and my life was turned upside down. It was now a couple of hours after threatening my platoon commander and I had already been to the base hospital and plans were in place to have me transferred to the closest military psych ward available. Another squad leader from my platoon met me and my wife at the hospital, basically to keep an eye on me to make sure I didn't do anything drastic, like run. I was then given time to go home and spend some time with her and pack some stuff before leaving.

The ride from Fort Huachuca, AZ to Fort Bliss, TX took about five hours. Three other soldiers were riding with me, basically guarding me to make sure I didn't try to escape or anything. Not one of them said a word to me the entire trip. I was no longer a soldier to them. I was no longer a brother. I was being escorted to a military psychiatric ward. To them, my time in the Army was over and I was of no use to them. I felt so empty during that ride. So lost. Confused. What the hell just happened? What just happened to my life? What's about to happen to my life? This would be my first ever visit to a psychiatric institution. I had no idea what to expect. My initial thoughts while riding in the van were that I was about to be put in a straight jacket, thrown in a padded room, and then fed pills and food through a tiny slot on my door. You know, what the movies portray. It was nothing like that.

After the initial paperwork and vitals, you're given a tour of the place by an actual Army soldier in the medical field. It was a U-shaped ward with the nurse's station located at the opened end of the 'U', our rooms were scattered around both sides along with a few activity rooms. It was located on one of the higher floors of the hospital, so if we tried to escape it would take us longer to get out of there. The first few days you are mostly confined to your room. You are not free to wander the ward because they want to monitor your mental state and see if you may be dangerous to others. After you pass this phase you're free to move about on your own in between scheduled classes and appointments. My first appointment was with a doctor who did the mental exams and cognitive tests. He gave me simple questions and gradually made them harder. He showed me pictures and paintings and asked me what I saw in them. He gave me a piece of paper and asked me to fold it as many times as I could. He asked me about what happened when I disobeyed and threatened my superiors and what I was thinking and feeling at the time.

I told him it felt like I had no control. That I knew everything I was doing was wrong but I had no ability to stop it. I told him I didn't realize the totality of what had just happened until many minutes after it happened. It's as if there was someone above me and they had strings attached to all of my limbs and they were playing me like a puppet. Every emotion and feeling, all of my senses were ripped and removed from my core. I felt empty, dry, rusted, worthless. He then asked about my past. This is when my brother and father came up. I told him the truth, about everything. Everything that I've already told you so far in this story. After about a week of tests and monitoring, the results came in.

"Mr. Hughes….."

Calling me Mr. Hughes instead of Sgt. Hughes really upset me and reminded me that everything I had worked so hard for was now gone. Forever. I was no longer allowed to be called by my rank. We wore our camouflage uniforms daily in the psych ward, but we were stripped of our rank. We were now civilians. And for me, that was the end. I had spent the last five years proving myself only to now be called 'Mr. Hughes'. It was a devastating blow in many ways. 'Mr.' was now a reminder that the last five years of my devotion to the military were all for naught.

Thanks for reminding me that I no longer have a purpose in life, Doc.

"Mr. Hughes, I'll explain all of these after I list them off. Severe depression. Obsessive-compulsive disorder. And bipolar mania. Now I'm sure you have an idea about what depression is…"

"But I don't feel depressed at all."

"A lot of people don't.", he replied.

"Mr. Hughes, I've done this for many years, decades even. I've gone over your charts and I've checked with the nurses about your routines here since you've been admitted. I've gone over your history. I've looked you in the eyes. You're depressed. And so depressed you don't even know that you're depressed. How you've made it this far without being diagnosed I have no idea."

This was the first time someone had looked me in the eyes and told me that something was wrong with me. That I'm different. That me and my brain are not normal. Just hearing that will make you depressed.

You're different.

You're not normal.

You've been unhappy for a long time.

Your bipolar mania was making you think you were happy.

You've lived the last few years according to your disorders, not according to you.

I'm sure those are hard things for a doctor to say to people on a daily basis. And they are definitely hard things to hear. My initial response after being told these things?

"Yeah right. Whatever, Doc. I don't believe any of that."

"Majority of people that come into my office usually don't.", he replied.

"OCD. Obsessive-compulsive disorder. From what I've gathered from you and others, you enjoy having things neat and clean. You've also admitted to sometimes counting your steps, or counting the lines in the middle of the road while you're driving. It has been reported to me by your superiors that you almost got into a wreck because you were counting those lines. Having things neat and clean is okay until it starts to interfere with normal daily routines. When compulsions and routines become more important than your necessities, you've encountered a problem."

I was definitely having problems. Very serious problems.

New Hampshire

He was right. I had always been a neat person. I washed my vehicle a lot. Cleaning the house more than I should. I checked the locks, windows, and oven burners every night before I went to bed. It all interfered with daily life. And the longer I went without treating it the worse it became. During my time at this unit, we participated in the usual mental ward stuff. We had classes and one-on-one therapy dealing with depression or whatever it was that we had been diagnosed with.

"Hi. My name is Jeremy and I have mental disorders."

"Hi, Jeremy."

You didn't have to talk if you didn't want to, but it was encouraged of course. I was always one to open up quickly. I've always hated uncomfortable silences. So when the person in charge of the class asked if anyone would like to share anything I would immediately start babbling. I didn't care what people thought. I wanted to figure out how to get out of that place. And if spilling my guts and confronting my problems would get me out sooner, well then that's what I was going to do. I cried many times in front of the others in my groups, mostly when bringing up how helpless you feel when the disorders take over. It's so demoralizing. I made others cry. Others made me cry. In my opinion, sitting in a room filled with people battling mental hardship is something that every person needs to experience at least once in their lifetime. That one meeting will change your opinion about mental disorders altogether.

The most free I have ever felt from my disorders was while I was in this psych ward. I fell from my chair onto my knees in a crying rage and spilled my guts trying to tell complete strangers how my disorders made me feel. Letting it all out, in my opinion, is one of the best things that you can do for yourself and your treatment. I highly recommend it. Even if you're alone and there's no one there to listen. Scream. Question everything. Slam your fists on the bed. Ball up on the floor and cry until you can hardly breathe. If anger is the only emotion you can generate and feel at that moment then generate it. Feel it. Try to maintain control of the emotions that you feel haven't already been taken from you, even if that emotion is anger.

As I've stated before, the hardest part for me was admitting I had a disorder. The second hardest part? Medications. Trying to find the right one. Dealing with the side effects of the previous medication wearing off while the side effects of the new medication kick in. Tremors. Weight gain. Weight loss. Hair loss. Headaches. Mood changes. Palpitations. Sweats. Insomnia. To name a few. It takes weeks and sometimes months for psychiatric medications to start performing properly. Please, if you are suffering from a mental illness, and you only take one thing from this story, let it be that. You have to know that it's going to take time. When you're pulled aside and told you have this or that problem and that you need to take certain medications, you have got to be patient. I beg you. You have to realize that you are trying to retrain the brain, the most sophisticated thing on the planet. It's not going to be fixed overnight. Not in a week. Not in a month. There is no set time frame to be cured. Just know that you *can* be cured.

But you have to keep trying. Sure the side effects can be terrible. Sure sometimes you feel worse off on the medication than you did before taking it. But I can't stress this enough, you have got to be patient with your medications, even with the side effects. Just because you have terrible side effects the first few days doesn't mean you will forever. For a lot of medications, the side effects wear off after a couple of weeks. After that, if you're still having problems then let your doctor know that you may need to try something else.

Don't feel like you have no say in your treatment. It is YOUR body. YOUR mind. Always listen to both. If something doesn't feel right then it probably isn't and you should let someone know. If you've given a medication a certain amount of time without any results then change the plan. But contact your doctor before immediately stopping any medication. You may need to be gradually weaned off of your current medicine. Please just be patient. Know that there are cures out there. Know that you are in control of finding that cure. You have a say. Don't just take the medication and feel like that's the only option and you have no say in your treatment.

The major depression isn't your fault. It's not sticking around because you can't get rid of it. It's not because you're weak. It's because the brain is extremely complex. The brain can perform around one thousand operations per second. Yes, one thousand. Now imagine you're battling something that complex. You aren't going to win that battle overnight. It's going to be a long battle. You are going to struggle. You are going to falter. You may even end up more depressed than you were before you're able to get a grasp on things. But don't blame yourself. It's not you. The majority of people with depression or any other mental disorder have the ability to overcome that disorder, or at least lessen the effects of it.

While at the Fort Bliss Psych Ward, I hit bottom. I was spilling my guts during an OCD group and I became extremely upset with the fact that I didn't have control over when to say enough cleaning was enough. That may seem minuscule to you, but not having control over anything is something no one likes. Here I sat in this room, coming to the conclusion that I had absolutely no control of any of my thoughts and decisions. When the thought of washing my car came to my mind, I washed it, even though I had just washed it the previous day. I had no power to say, "you know what, I don't need to wash my car, it's clean." No power at all.

When my depression hit, it was the same. No power to be happy. No control to not be sad. I was at the mercy of the disorder. And it is a very terrible way to go through life. But you can overcome it. I've done it a couple of times. You can overcome your sadness. You can overcome checking the doorknobs three times a night before you go to bed. Trust me, you can. You have to tell yourself that you can. If you try to tell yourself that you can and that intrusive thought of, "no you can't" enters your mind instead, that's your disorder speaking, not you. You have to realize that. We are not wired to generate intrusive and controlling thoughts like that. Know that you are meant to be a happy person. You are meant to go about your days and through life without being held down by mental hardships.

Sure there are things in life that happen that will make you unhappy. A friend moves away. Your pet dies. You lose your job. Those are all things that may happen to you and anyone. But for some people, something like that can send a person into a major, deep depression. Why? Because that person's brain is wired to do so.

AND THAT'S OKAY!

Alaska

It's okay to not be perfect! It's okay to have a flaw. It's okay to have to seek the help of someone else to get through a trying time. Whether that person is a friend or a doctor or whoever. Don't worry about the stigma or what others are going to say. Are you seriously going to put aside your overall health and happiness because you don't want your coworkers or friends to know you may have depression? Almost sixty million Americans suffer from a mental illness. So some of your coworkers and friends are most likely suffering as well. Why give anyone the satisfaction of controlling your decisions and your overall health? YOU need satisfaction. You need relaxation. Your brain needs to rest. YOU need to rest. Get help! If someone comes up to you or pulls you aside and acts genuinely concerned and offers help because they can see that you may be having a problem, TAKE THEIR HELP.

"I don't mean to intrude into your personal life, but you just seem a bit off lately. Is everything okay?"

Let it out!

"NO, I'M NOT OKAY! PLEASE HELP ME!"

Even if you have no clue what's wrong, accept their offer of help.

Do not take that offer for help as an insult. You need to realize that that person may see something you don't. Or they see something you see and just want to help. The fact of the matter is that it's extremely hard to overcome any mental disorder. It's even harder to do it by yourself. Don't be ashamed to let someone know that you may be struggling with something, even if you don't know what that something is. Every person on this earth struggles just about every single day. Struggle is a part of life. Some people struggle more than others. When those struggles happen to someone with a mental disorder, the struggles are extremely amplified. You may be upset that rush hour traffic is taking forever to move along. But the person in the car next to you is glad it's taking forever. Why? Because that person is going home to a darkened living room with the phone and TV turned off and will ball up on the couch and cry and not move until the next morning. And then they will wake up the next day and do the same routine all over again. Why will they do that? Because their disorders have them thinking that that's normal. That hiding and not acknowledging the problem is okay. Mental illnesses can be very evil in the way they manipulate you, your thoughts, and your emotions.

Once the disorder takes control of your routines you're pretty much at rock bottom. The disorder has full reign. Whatever thoughts the disorder puts into your head, you do, without hesitation. It tells you you're supposed to be sad, and you do it.

It tells you to hide in your home away from others, so you do it. It tells you to go buy twenty pairs of socks even though you already have an entire drawer full. It tells you to bawl your eyes out because an old lady on the news got scammed by her mechanic. It tells you to not laugh at things that used to make you laugh. That's not you choosing not to laugh. That's the disorder controlling what you laugh at.

There is happiness still inside of you. It's just been covered up. The ability to recognize that happiness has been taken from you. A mental wall has been built to keep you from seeing and taking part in that happiness. And you have to realize that you didn't lose that ability because you were weak or incapable. You lost that ability because you have a mental disorder. There are nerves and signals in your brain that aren't firing correctly.

AND THAT'S OKAY!

You will be happy. You will get control. You will admit you have a disorder. You will seek help. You will be patient with your treatment. You will take control of your treatment. You will listen to your body, not the intrusive thoughts of your mind. You will get back on track. You will regain control of your decisions and emotions. You will be you. It took me a long time to finally be me again and to be able to live comfortably with my mental disorders, almost twenty-one years. Well maybe I'm not 100% me yet mentally, but I am in control these days. I will live with these disorders for the rest of my life. I have accepted them. Years ago I sat face-to-face with a doctor and he looked me in the eye and told me that I would be in an uphill mental battle for the rest of my life.

Do you know where the term 'uphill battle' comes from? It's a military term of course. When you attack an enemy that is perched on a hill, you not only have to attack, but you also have to climb, making your chances of winning the battle almost impossible. Your disorder is relaxing at the top of that hill in a hammock, rolling boulders down the hill toward every corner of your mind, while you struggle to just find footing for your next step up. The turf will give and you'll slip and fall back down the hill. You'll regain your footing, and make it halfway back up, only to be knocked down by another boulder. But, there will be times when your treatment plan will come into alignment and you'll gain a tactical advantage. Over time, these advantages will happen more often, until your disorder falls out of its hammock and down the hill. It's during these moments that you must remain proactive with your treatment. Just because you're feeling great and your depression or mania doesn't seem to be bothering you, doesn't mean you should stop your daily therapy and treatment routines.

REALIZATION ACCEPTANCE TREATMENT PATIENCE

Do these four things and you will conquer. I guarantee it.

Yes, some people are so enthralled by their disorder that 'realization' is almost impossible. And sometimes it takes those around you to help you come to that realization. Hopefully, you'll come to decipher how to realize it. How to pinpoint what's normal and what's not. You know you're sad. You know you've been depressed longer than normal. If you know that then you know something isn't right. You've just realized you have a problem, realize that you need help. I told you those intrusive thoughts are not of your own making. When you go home and curl up on the couch and shun the outside world every day, that's not you making that choice, that's your disorder making that choice for you. REALIZE IT. ACCEPT IT. You have a disorder. You have an illness. You're not perfect. You have a problem within your mind that is not of your own doing. TREAT IT. Stop worrying about what everyone else might think. The majority of the people who may judge you for your disorder most likely have a disorder themselves. It's a statistical fact. Stop hiding from it. Stop setting it aside. You've been through enough.

Putting it off and hoping things get better on their own is the worst thing you can do.

If you can't afford treatment, don't stop there. Many places will offer help for free. If you can't find help, usually your local health department is the best place to start. They should be able to lead you in the right direction. PATIENCE. You will not get better overnight. You need to realize this and accept this as soon as possible. While waiting for your medications and such to start working, I recommend Cognitive Behavioral Therapy, breathing techniques, and meditation. And two of the most important things you can do for your brain is to eat right and exercise. You don't have to have a healthy meal three times a day. Just add some healthier items here and there. As far as exercise goes, a simple thirty-minute walk every day will work. Get out of your house and breathe in some fresh air. Crack a window and turn a fan on. You may be surprised how stuffy your home actually is. Change the filter on your HVAC unit. Clean air inside your body can do amazing things.

It will work wonders.

I know what you're saying to yourself. "Eating? Walking? Fresh air? Those are going to help me? Get the hell out of here!" I said the same thing when numerous doctors told me that. But then I thought, if numerous doctors are all telling me the same things, there must be some truth to it. Did I start eating better and exercising right away? Of course not. Because I thought something so minuscule wouldn't help in the uphill battle I was engaged in. Today, those three things have proven to be great weapons.

Cognitive behavioral therapy also requires patience, as you are teaching the brain new routines and behaviors. Eventually, after doing this therapy every day, the brain picks up on these routines and begins to do what you are trying to teach it. It is a scheduled pattern that you create. There is no standard pattern. There are many CBT apps available. Also download Prana Breath, or a similar breathing app. Find a quiet place and do some breathing exercises for a few minutes at a time a few times a day. And finally, the most important thing you can do in the fight against your disorder? Absolutely nothing. And by nothing I mean SLEEP. Sleep is as important as diet and exercise. Good sleep helps your overall brain performance and moods.

From the National Institute of Health
"Studies show that sleep deficiency changes activity in some parts of the brain. If you're sleep deficient, you may have trouble making decisions, solving problems, controlling your emotions and behavior, and coping with change. Sleep

deficiency has also been linked to depression, suicide, and risk-taking behavior."

Don't just rely on medication and therapy sessions. There are many things you can do at home to improve your mental well-being. Take control of your treatment. Take control of your body. Take control of your mind. Take control of you. Walk, eat healthier, and remove stressors from your life. But don't do too much at one time. You're already overwhelmed with whatever it is you're going through. Take your time in treating yourself. Be patient with yourself. Before beginning any treatment or uphill climb to get better, you MUST tell yourself that it is going to take time. Lots of time. If you expect positive results right away you are just setting yourself up for failure.

Hey, you. You can do this. Be patient.

North Dakota

I know I went a little off course with that last chapter, but that's what came to mind at the time. My treatment at the Fort Bliss psych ward was very helpful. But I left in denial. I learned a lot while I was there and the staff were very professional and great at helping me understand many things. They explained to us what these disorders are, what they do, and helped us learn ways to treat them. But my demon was now out. Halfway through my time there I spiraled out of control and lost all touch with reality. I was in a daze most of the day. I stopped participating in group therapy and I went silent during one-on-one sessions. My medications were increased but it was too late. Nothing at this institution was going to stop it.

I of course was released and sent back home in this mental state. A short time after returning to Fort Huachuca there was some kind of medical situation with my wife's grandmother, which I mentioned before. On top of that, she and I had already been seeing a post chaplain for couples therapy. So with that, and after what just happened to me, it was safe to say our relationship was pretty much over. Military life just wasn't for her. In the beginning, she took it really hard. Considering it was her first time being away from home I'd have to say she did really well. She toughed it out and tried her best, and military life eventually grew on her and things became easier. But it just wasn't meant to be. We had an amicable split.

I remember taking her to the airport so she could go see her grandmother, I knew that was probably the last time I would see her for a long time. What I didn't realize, until on the ride back home, was that I was now alone, except for the demon of course. Once I returned home from the airport he wasted no time in letting me know that it was his time to shine.

Waiting for my medical review board to be finalized was hell. For those who don't know, military medical review boards can take many months to process. It's basically the military's version of a social security judge determining your disabilities. I suffered a few injuries while in the Army so they had to review everything to determine what they were at fault for and how much to pay me when discharged. Once I was back in Arizona from Fort Bliss, I was reassigned to the Select Honor Guard, a position I had already been in and loved. I was sent back to the Honor Guard the second time because after threatening my lieutenant I was no longer allowed to hold a weapon. I was useless in a tactical sense.

My two stints in the Honor Guard were, at the time, my shining moments in life. I excelled. I took the worst-performing squad and eventually made them the best. My soldiers looked up to me. I was stern with my training style but respectful. I respected them, and they appreciated that.

We had many cookouts and gatherings together after work. It was such a great time. As an Honor Guard squad, we performed burial ceremonies for veterans, participated in parades, and presented our nation's colors during balls and change of command ceremonies. It was so awesome to me. The precision and technicalities it took to perform these duties enthralled me. I was addicted to the job.

But my demon was coming full tilt. He needed to go. He couldn't take anymore of being cramped up in that tiny house on base waiting forever to be released. He needed to hit the road. And so did I. I should have still been in the psych ward at Fort Bliss. Each day that went by after my wife left was another day of me being alone with a disorder that was about to take complete control over my life. In the coming weeks, OCD would be the first thing to show its ugly face and be the driving force behind everything I did. The hours after work that I had to myself were spent cleaning. Then re-cleaning. Then cleaning again. By the time everything was triple-cleaned, it was time to quadruple-clean the first thing I cleaned.

I was using hand sanitizer on a daily basis before Covid made it cool to do so. Bacteria and other people's germs coming into contact with any part of my body was instant hell. I may as well have been walking around and going to work in a bio-hazard suit. Still to this day, I use hand sanitizer before and after pumping gas. Take a second and think about how nasty those gas pump handles are with hundreds of people touching them every day. Now take a second and realize that they never get cleaned.

Gross huh?

My OCD would get worse and worse. I would count my steps when entering buildings and would keep a log book of how many steps for each building I went into. I was now checking the oven knobs, door locks, and window latches even more times than before. I couldn't relax and get comfortable enough in bed to fall asleep if these rituals were not done. It reached its pinnacle when I found myself sitting on the kitchen floor with all of the canned goods surrounding me. I would organize them by product. Alphabetize them. And when placing them back in the cabinets the labels had to be facing forward.

I probably did this a few times a week for a couple of months. Then one day the OCD immediately came to an end and the bipolar mania inside me awoke. Theft. The first thing that was stolen was a street sign. Hughes St. My last name. This was a street *on* the military base of Fort Huachuca. So not only am I stealing, but I'm stealing federal property. Of course, coming up with a plan and actually stealing the sign was a huge rush for me. But it only lasted so long.

Now before I share the next little tidbit, let's remember that bipolar has just struck and taken over, I've spent the last five years ignoring my father's death and depression is beginning to seep out of every part of my body, my wife just left and is most likely not coming back, and my family is 1,256 miles away. Not that it mattered. I didn't have the mental ability to even recognize what was going on, let alone call someone for help. After stealing the street sign, the next ridiculous thing I remember doing was going to the Sierra Vista Mall and testing each department store's loss prevention team.

Yes, I actually went to department stores one by one and intentionally looked like a shoplifter to see if anyone would confront me. No one did, except Dillard's.

"Sir, are you okay?"

"Yes, I am. Why?"

"Well, you've been staring at these belts for almost twenty minutes now."

"Actually it's been twenty-two minutes. You should have interacted with me much sooner."

After I told him what I was doing this guy brought me back to their loss prevention office to discuss what I saw and what I thought could help their loss prevention team. I wasn't in there long. I remember telling him that one of their fire escape doors opened up to a parking lot exit, making a getaway easy. They thanked me for the "help" and I went on my way.

I did ridiculous stuff like this for about a month until stealing more stuff got the better of me.

Maryland

After stealing the street sign, I needed something more challenging. When my mania kicks in it's all about feeding the rush.

"Hi there. Can I help you?"

"Yes. I'm interested in this Pontiac Grand Prix."

"Do you mind if I ask if you know what your credit is like?"

I gave the young salesman a devilish grin. "Doesn't matter."

"How's that?"

"I just won the lottery. My bank on base has a hold on the transfer from the state lottery office so I'm just browsing in advance. I'll take this one."

The car salesman took me inside and drew up the paperwork right then and there. He didn't give me the keys right then, that would be insane and he'd probably get fired. But he drew up the sales receipt and everything. All that needed to be done was to wait for the hold to be lifted on the lottery money that I had never won.

Now imagine for a second how messed up the wires in my brain had to have been to patiently sit there in that car dealership knowing that I had no way of paying for this car. Yet I waited for him to draw up this paperwork and then walked out the door like I was ever coming back to pay. How insane is that? If you have ever bought a car at a dealership then you know it's a 1 1/2 hour process, minimum. This is how in control my demon was. This is how in control your demon can get, and without you even knowing it. Total and complete control. Whatever thought my messed up mind produced, it seemed like the best thought at that time, and I never questioned any of them. I had no power to dissect whether or not it was a good or bad decision. I just did what my mind told me to do. Manic episodes of bipolar, at their worst, can be very devastating and crippling. Once you are in the deepest depths of a manic episode it usually takes a support group to get you out of it.

A few days after leaving the dealership I woke up and got dressed to go to work. I got in the car, backed down the driveway, stopped to look both ways to see if any traffic was coming, and to my left I saw a Pontiac Grand Prix parked on the curb. Yes, *that* Pontiac Grand Prix. I signed the paperwork agreeing to pay and those idiots delivered the car to my home *on base* and left it there. It was now my financial responsibility.

It was now my ride out of here. Why? Because my superiors knew the make, model, and license plate of my actual car. They knew nothing about this car. They wouldn't know what to look for to find me. The little devil was very evil. But also very smart.

Prior to hopping in the Grand Prix and running, I stole something else. As a squad leader in the Honor Guard, I had access to all of the training tools and equipment at our facility. I ended up stealing a very valuable camera that we used to record our performances so we could watch and review them to see what we could improve on. This was a $600 camera. The rush was great but only lasted for so long. A few days after stealing the camera I walked in to work and it immediately felt like everyone was staring at me. And they were. I walked up to a few members of my squad to ask what was going on and they whispered to me that they couldn't talk at the moment and turned away.

What the hell was going on?

I made my way towards our platoon sergeant's office and another squad leader stepped in front of me and told me I wasn't allowed to enter at the moment. I turned and looked around and decided to go outside for a cigarette. Two soldiers quickly blocked the doorway to prevent me from going outside. At this point, I was extremely frustrated. My top blew.

I turned towards everyone and yelled as loud as I could.

"What the hell is going on?!"

"Sgt. Hughes! My office! Now!"

I turned towards my platoon sergeant's office to see him fuming. I walked over and into his office with the most confused look on my face. He slammed the door, walked to his desk and ordered me to sit down. I refused. He then went on to inform me that one of the cameras had been stolen. He then asked me if I had taken it.

"No, Sergeant."

"Are you sure? This is your chance. Did you steal the camera?"

"No, Sergeant. I borrowed it. I have no reason to steal anything. I took it to study film while at home because I couldn't figure out how to get the memory card out of it. So I took the whole thing so I could just hook it up to my computer with a cord and watch the recordings that way. I guess I just forgot to turn it back in. I have it at home. I swear there was no intention of stealing. I own a personal camera and have no need for that one."

Of course, this was all a huge lie. Unfortunately, at this point, I needed a constant rush to feed my mania. Even if it was the rush of lying.

"Let's go get it.", he said.

We got in his truck and I directed him to my home across the base. When we arrived there were already two Criminal Investigation cars waiting. I unlocked the door but wasn't allowed in. They proceeded to search my entire home even though I told them that the camera was on the desk in the living room. While searching they also found the street sign I had stolen. I was handcuffed and driven to the post jail on two counts of theft of federal property. I was booked and processed and put in a cell. Two hours later I was released.

Once my attorney showed up I informed her that I admitted to taking the camera for training purposes and had no intention of stealing it. I also informed her that when I entered the Honor Guard facility I wasn't allowed to leave. I then told her that they searched my entire home without a warrant and did not read me any rights.

False imprisonment. Illegal search of property. No Miranda rights.

I was immediately let go with no charges.

The demon had won again.

South Carolina

After being arrested and released, I was no longer allowed to work any job in the military. I was stripped of my Honor Guard duties. I now had no job, at all. I simply had to report to physical training every morning and then go back home. This was my daily routine until my medical review was finalized. My mania was now at a supercharged level. Being in my home all day with absolutely no reason to face the next day was the saddest and most excruciating point in my life. I lived on the couch. The TV never came on. I didn't shower. I didn't eat. The worthlessness I felt is indescribable. I lasted a few weeks in this condition until I couldn't take it anymore and decided to make my escape. Well, the disorder decided. I can't recall why I stayed there for that long after my Honor Guard position was taken from me. But the car dealership paperwork and the day I showed up back home in Arkansas prove I stayed on base in Arizona for a few weeks after receiving the car and before hitting the road.

Now, we are at the beginning of the escapade. You've made it to the part where I lose complete control, of everything. The part where I give in to my demon one hundred percent. I am now my demon. I am a demon. I have given you an overview in previous chapters of what's about to happen but it's now time for the terrible, albeit, juicy details.

On Saturday, December 14th, 2002, at about 3 a.m., I grabbed the dog, some clothes, and food, and I drove out of the gates of Fort Huachuca, AZ, never to see them again. I intentionally left my bipolar medications behind because I DID NOT HAVE MENTAL ISSUES! I did of course, but the little guy on my shoulder told me I didn't, and I listened to everything he said.

If you have ever driven west of the Dallas/Fort Worth area then you know there is absolutely nothing there. There is no scenery to look at except oil rigs, dust, and desert. It is the worst driving scenery imaginable. And it never ends. The road just goes on and on. It was the worst trip I have ever made in my life. Ever! Sorry, I had to get that out of my system. The worst! Okay, I'm done. But, on this particular trip, it was all amazing. As soon as I hit the freeway and headed east out of Arizona I felt a huge weight come off of my shoulders. I could breathe easier. The air was crisp and clean going down into my lungs. I had a smile on my face. The oil rigs were intriguing. The desert was beautiful. I was free from everything, except my mind of course.

But in all honesty, there was no weight lifted. I couldn't breathe easier. The air was not crisp and clean. I didn't have a smile on my face. The oil rigs were not intriguing. And I was not free. It was all a ruse constructed by my mind. That's what mental disorders do. They cloud reality. They think for you.

They make you decide things without thinking them through. They make you feel things that you aren't feeling. They force a smile on your face while you're dying inside. They put a mirage over your eyes and your mind. They project a mood of comfort and contentment, while at the same time, your mind is going 100 mph. So fast that you can't even concentrate on one single thought that's flashing by.

And remember, NONE OF THAT IS YOUR FAULT!

Bipolar manic episodes are not fun. They can even be dangerous, especially if you don't get help soon enough. The reason they are dangerous is because you don't eat much. You don't sleep. At all. And on top of no sleep, you feel like you have everlasting energy and can do anything for any amount of time. Non-stop. All day and all night, for many days at a time. You have no idea how tired you are because your mind continues to push you to find the next rush until it's too late and you fall out from exhaustion and/or dehydration. It's a terrible disorder.

It's seventeen hours from Ft. Huachuca to central Arkansas. I was so manic I did it in one straight shot. I stopped for one little nap. But besides that, I was on the move. My bipolar had me so wound up that I couldn't stop. I couldn't stop if I wanted to because I was no longer in control of what was happening to me. I remember crying while flying down the freeway because I had absolutely no control over what I was doing. No clue where I was going. I couldn't get off at an exit if I wanted to. My mind wouldn't allow it. I was falling apart emotionally, crumbling, realizing I was now AWOL from the military and on the run from the military and Sierra Vista police. I had no clue how long the car dealership waited before they contacted the authorities or my superiors on base. It didn't matter. I was long gone and out of their jurisdiction.

I drove and drove, with no clue where I was going exactly. I knew I was going back to my old stomping grounds of central Arkansas. But I had no clue where I was going or what I was going to tell everyone once I arrived. It was around 8 p.m. on Saturday, December 14th, 2002. The Christmas holiday service was ending when I stepped through the front doors of my old church in Sherwood, AR.

I had to call my mother to get the details about this particular part of the story. I couldn't remember how I knew everyone was there or why I decided to go to the church. I called her while writing this chapter and she informed me that a few days before I left Arizona I had called her to tell her that I won the lottery. That's how messed up I was! I believed my demon so much that I called my mother and told her this ridiculous story that my demon had concocted. She of course did not believe anything I said. It was during that phone call that she told me about the Christmas service at the church, which is how I knew where everyone was and where to go once I got back to central Arkansas.

Now you have to picture this in detail. I just drove from Arizona to Arkansas in about seventeen hours in a stolen car. No sleep. No overnight hotel stay. Nothing. I was so wired. I probably looked and acted like I was on crack. I walked right into the church as if none of that was happening to me. As if I belonged there. I smiled and said hello to church members I hadn't seen in years. I talked with a few friends from my youth group days. Then my mother spotted me as she was walking from one part of the church to another. The look she gave me was one of extreme concern. She knew immediately that something was terribly wrong. And I immediately knew that she knew. I don't remember talking to her, although I'm sure we did have some kind of conversation. I just don't remember what we said if we did talk. I ended up leaving the church with my wife. Although, at that point, she and I were separated, just…not officially. I stayed with her that night at her friend's house where she was living at the time.

I never went to the house where my mother and brothers were staying. It never crossed my mind. That thought probably wasn't allowed to cross my mind. They most likely would have ended the ridiculous endeavor I was on. There was no way my mind was going to allow them to do that. I involuntarily steered clear of them at all costs once I left the church. That was the last place my mind wanted to be. It was the only place *I* wanted to be.

That place was so close, yet so far away.

Montana

Please forgive me as some exact time frames of certain events have been forgotten. I remember the majority of things that took place during this manic episode fiasco. But some exact times and periods of the day have since escaped my mind. Not only does the manic episode and the disorder itself make it hard to remember things, but it's also hard to list everything chronologically. As I type this very sentence, it is April 22, 2023, over twenty years since all of this happened. So time is also a factor in not remembering pin-point details, but I will do my best.

As good as I can remember, I think I spent the first two nights back in Arkansas with my ex-wife. I know I spent that Saturday night with her, I'm just not sure about the next night. I do know that on the morning of December 16th, 2002, is when I decided to continue my crime spree further. And for some reason, I wanted to go visit my grandfather, my father's father. Why I chose to go see him I have no idea. But I woke up that day and it was my first thought. Growing up I had a good relationship with him. I spent many summers doing yard work and cleaning the pool for him and my grandmother.

I always admired his work ethic and military service. Maybe that's why he was the second person I went to see once I got back home, that military connection.

I left my ex-wife's place and drove from North Little Rock, AR to Jacksonville, AR to visit him and let him know that my military service was up and that I was back home, neither of which were true of course. He was really happy to see me and welcomed me inside. He sat at the bar that faced the kitchen and I made myself comfortable on the couch. We talked about my time in the Army, everywhere I had been, and things I had seen and experienced. He of course shared some great stories about his time in the military and I soaked them up like I had just been granted the ability to hear. I think he was eighty-one at this point, so it took him a while to remember things and get his stories across. But even with my mania so wound up, I was more than content to sit there and listen to stories about his past. That is until he got up to use the restroom. Now, at his age, he was not getting around well at all. He was a healthy man. Tall and built like a boulder. And he could still do everything on his own. But he now moved very slowly. And unfortunately for him, the demon noticed this. As soon as he shut the door to the restroom the little devil took over.

"He's gone now and will be for a while. Take that giant jar of money over there. Now!"

I waited a moment after he shut the door then jumped up and went over to the fireplace. Next to it was a giant pickle jar. I'm talking about the old ones that are about two feet tall with the wooden lid. That jar had been there forever. Many years. And it was filled to the brim with coins and bills. Money for a rainy day. Lots of rainy days. And boy was I having a rainy day. Ten years prior, in my mid-teens, I would be enthralled by that jar every time we'd visit my grandparents. Now here I was, twenty-five years old, about to steal it. Without hesitation, I picked up that giant jar and loaded it into the car.

"Now, go back in and find something else to take that will benefit us. Do it! Now!"

And I did just that. I went back in and looked for anything else I could take, knowing he would be a little while longer in the bathroom. I scoured the bar and found two checkbooks which I immediately grabbed up. I knew the layout of this house well but I didn't have time to do a walk-through of the entire place. He moved slowly, but not *that* slow. So I had to focus my theft on the living room and dining areas. I searched through all of the shelves and flipped through papers on the bar. I peeked into his room which was next to the living room. I found his wallet but there was nothing inside. Not finding anything else, and knowing I didn't have much more time, I left, leaving my grandfather alone and confused.

I just stole three things from my grandfather. Three more felonies. I now had four of them, the other being grand theft auto. In just three days I was AWOL from the Army and had racked up four felonies. I had completely sent my mother spiraling and just stole from a man I had admired my entire life and had nothing but respect for. I had never stolen anything in my entire life! Nothing! I mean, not that I know of. I may have taken something that didn't belong to me when I was a kid, but as an adult, I had never taken anything that wasn't mine, besides the street sign and camera I had stolen at Fort Huachuca of course. And I just did it towards my own blood. And then I left him there, alone and confused as to what had just happened. It's so sad to think of how he must have felt. So helpless. It brings me so much pain to think of him coming out of that bathroom to nothing. I went there to surprise him and let him know that I was "back home and out of the Army". Instead, I turned that warm, family moment into theft in the blink of an eye. I feel so ashamed looking back on that moment.

I had absolutely no intention of doing any of that to him. It never crossed my mind on the way to his home. I was enjoying seeing him and he seemed to be glad I chose to come see him and to see how he was doing. The visit was great, with a welcoming hug and great conversation. And in an instant, my disorder reminded me who was in charge. Not even halfway down his street, I had a smile on my face. A smile I didn't want to smile. I had just committed three felonies against a family member and was on the run from the law. It never crossed my mind that anything I had just done was at all bad. I couldn't have gone back and returned the stuff if I wanted to. I didn't have the mental power to create such a thought. And even if I *could* create that thought, what would I say?

"Hey, Granddaddy. Me again. Sorry about leaving in a rush like that. I stole your big jar of change and two checkbooks. But I got to the end of your neighborhood and decided to bring them back. Here ya go."

I was at the mercy of my mind. When these manic episodes hit, most of the time you don't even know it until it's too late. This was my first extreme manic episode. I had just robbed my grandfather and felt nothing but excitement after doing it. Complete rush. The rush was so great that it overshadowed the illegal ramifications of what I had just done. How this would affect my grandfather was a thought that never entered my mind. The ability to decipher what I had just done and how it may have affected him did not exist.

At that point, my soul did not exist.

Idaho

Stealing from my grandfather unfortunately filled me with a ton of criminal adrenaline. I wanted more of that feeling. I needed more of that feeling. If I could have had that feeling injected into me I would have sold what was left of my soul to feel it again. I needed more money to fund this pathetic escapade. What I had taken from my grandfather wasn't in the best spendable form. And this was 2002, so there weren't coin machines in Wal-Mart where I could take this giant jar to cash it in. I needed actual cash. Ah ha! The checkbooks. First Arkansas Bank & Trust here I come! A quick forge of a $200 check by using his signature from the carbon copy of the previous check he wrote and I'm in the money! I filled in the 'for' section with 'yard work'. I remember making sure to write it for a small amount to not bring attention to it. It worked. A few minutes later I'm pulling out of the bank drive-thru with $200 in cash. Bingo!

"Go to another bank branch and do it again. Now!"

I'm on it.

I made my way to the main branch in downtown Jacksonville, AR. This particular incident is when local authorities would be brought into the picture. My demon was getting greedy. But I always did what my demon said. And I did it without hesitation. For some reason, I went inside this branch instead of using the drive-thru. I really can't recall why. From a criminal standpoint, going into that bank was the worst decision I had made so far. Morally, the worst decision would be stealing from my grandfather. But let me repaint this moment for you. I had just forged a check across town. And a few minutes later I was sitting in a stolen car, with stuff I had stolen from my grandfather, and I was forging another one of his checks, this time for $500. How insane is that? This is what bipolar can do to you. Within days it can turn your life upside down before you have any kind of chance to defend yourself from it.

I casually made my way inside and waited in line for the next teller. I'm sure I looked like some nervous, homeless guy hyped up on the latest designer drug. But to me, I felt like the other side of the pillow. Everything seemed great. Life was grand. It hadn't been thirty minutes since I had left my grandfather's house, yet here I was grinning ear to ear knowing I was about to have more of his cash placed in my hands. There was no shame at all for what I had just done to him. That emotion no longer existed in my brain. I presented the check to the teller and provided my I.D. After punching a few buttons into her computer she excused herself to double-check something. At this moment I am totally cool. I'm calm and collected, for a couple of minutes. Then those couple of minutes turned into five minutes. I then looked into the office behind the counter where the teller went and noticed she was showing the check to someone else.

Now I'm not the sharpest spoon in the drawer, but if you have your own office at a bank then I assume you're some kind of manager or financial officer. Now that a person in charge was in the mix I knew something wasn't right and that I needed to make my escape. And I needed to do it immediately. I didn't turn and run or initiate any kind of drastic getaway that might cause a scene. I just casually leaned over and asked the next teller for directions to the bathroom. She kindly informed me that they were just near the entrance. I thanked her and made my way towards the restrooms but instead walked right out of the bank. I had been made. I would find out later on during an interrogation that the Jacksonville Police Department had already been called while I was standing in line waiting for the lady who had gone to the back office. From the time I pulled out of the parking lot to the time they showed up was a matter of seconds. With those two forgeries, I now had six felonies tallied up, five of which were against my grandfather.

Can we take another second and let that sink in? My own grandfather! I can't stop shaking my head while typing this. I feel so sad for him. I've never forgiven myself for these things, even though I know it wasn't really me doing all of this terrible stuff to all of these people. Later, after this entire escapade was over, I would also learn that the smaller bank that I went to first did not yet have the new digital signature software for checks. The main branch had this software. And when the teller from that branch scanned the check the software did not accept the forgery, which is why she took it to the manager's office. But by then I was long gone.

I needed to get somewhere, and fast. I needed to get out of the area and off of the road. But where could I go? By now my grandfather had probably called my mother trying to figure out what happened to me. The Jacksonville police now had my identity through the bank cameras and they probably also had the make and model of my car through exterior cameras. I needed to disappear. By now, the majority of people who knew me know what's going on. Most everyone knows that I'm AWOL from the Army and that I'm in a stolen vehicle.

I have to leave this area and I have to do it now.

But first....

"Go to your mother's work and show her the sales receipt for the car to prove to her that you did win the lottery and you bought the car with the winnings. Go! Now!"

I'm on it. Headed there now.

My demon steered the car across Jacksonville to the store that she managed. I walked in and asked for her but she wasn't there at the moment. I left the sales receipt for the car on the counter and walked out. I was so far in the depths of my manic episode that I believed that this would prove that everything I told her about winning the lottery was true. Everyone I came into contact with must have thought I was out of my mind. And I was. While leaving the parking lot of her work I noticed her pulling in. I don't know if she noticed me or not.

I didn't stop. I missed her so much. I was missing myself. I wish I could have just parked the car and given her a big hug and begged her to take me somewhere for help. But at that moment I was under the impression I didn't need help. I was a prisoner of my mind. And my mind told me I needed to hit the road before I was caught.

I headed south on Highway 67/167 out of Jacksonville towards Little Rock, AR. Where was I going? I had no clue. I was now on the run from the Jacksonville, AR police, the military police, and the Sierra Vista, AZ police.

I was also on the run from myself.

Illinois

While driving towards Little Rock I started running through the list of people I knew in the area that may not have an idea of what's going on with me, and that live a good distance from central Arkansas. I needed to be as far away as possible from any big city. And the opposite of a big city is a small country town. The first town that came to my mind was Monticello, Arkansas. That delightful place where I grew up on the farm and experienced so many wonderful times. Why I immediately thought of Monticello I have no idea. But while sitting here writing this I think I just naturally drove there.

It was almost as if wonderful memories of my past took me there. Past happiness and comfort steered my car in that direction I think. While enduring the worst part of my life, somehow my mind decided to comfort me and send me to the place where I spent the best part of my life. I think this was when my mind started trying to fight back. It knew I couldn't fight on my own. Call me crazy but I really believe going to Monticello was my mind and body trying to battle what had come over me. I was so lost in every aspect, yet I drove to the place that instilled so much happiness into my life. I only knew two people that were still living there. One of them was my father's first wife, and there was no way I was going to go see her. She is one of the nicest and sweetest people you'd ever meet, but she was too immediate of a family member and may have known what was going on with me. The other person I knew there was my wife's cousin.

She had been a bridesmaid in our wedding two years prior. She had her own place, probably didn't know anything about what was going on with me, and would most likely welcome me and let me stay until I figured out a more permanent place to rest my head. She was of course shocked to see me. I don't remember her asking too many questions about why I was there or anything like that. She was always so nice. She opened up her home to me. I remember going to the local Wal-Mart to buy coin rollers so I could roll all of the coins I had stolen from my grandfather and cash them in. I sat on her couch and rolled and rolled. I got a lot of them rolled but not enough to make a trip into a bank worth it. I'm sure I made up some ridiculous lies about why I was there and where I had gotten the huge jar that was now sitting on her floor.

There I sat, making casual conversation and just enjoying the moment and my escape earlier that day. The rush of almost being caught had provided a confusing but welcomed comfort. There she sat, chatting with her cousin's husband, having no clue a felon running from the law was in her home. As good as I can recall, I stayed with her for two nights, maybe only one. I couldn't afford to stay in one place for too long. At least not until I found a more safe and desolate place to call home. Was I running away for good? I think at this point I had no choice. What the hell was I doing? I was a convicted felon on the run. My God, what was happening to me?

On the morning of December 18th(I'm pretty sure), I left her home and drove the one hour back to Jacksonville. Why was I going back to the scene of the crimes? Because I'm in the darkest depths of a bipolar manic episode and I'm completely at its mercy. The ability to doubt any thought that entered my mind was long gone. Any stupid ideation my mind generated was immediately considered the only way to go about things. I would find out later after all of this was over that my older brother CJ had created flyers asking about my whereabouts and they had placed them all over Jacksonville. So not only were the authorities looking for me, but there were pictures of me all over the place. My family knew I was far from okay and were extremely concerned. They are such a wonderful family and I would not be here writing this today if it weren't for them.

I was going back to where I had just committed my most recent crimes. Can you believe that? Right back to where I had just stolen from my grandfather and forged his checks. Days earlier I had escaped being caught by mere seconds, yet here I was right back in the middle of Jacksonville, which is not a big city at all. What could possibly be there that would benefit me and be worth the risk knowing that the local police were looking for me?

Knowledge.

I knew this town. It's where I spent my teenage years. I knew people here. I needed money. I needed shelter. And I needed that rush to keep my mania going. And if I had to get those things back in Jacksonville then damn it that's what I was going to do. I did not think twice about this decision. It was the most beneficial place for me at the time. Right now, as I write this, I can see how crazy it was to go back. At that moment in time, I didn't have the ability to recognize how crazy it was. Again, this is what bipolar does. It's as if it forces another human into you. You take on the role of a different person. It's like getting up on a stage to portray a character in a play and you involuntarily continue to be that character once the play is over.

Another thing that stands out to me about all of this is that while I was doing all of this stuff, my future didn't matter. It never crossed my mind. Just a few months prior I was this person who was hell-bent on knowing his purpose and knowing what his future held. I was never comfortable unless I had some kind of knowledge as to where I was at in life, or where I was going. I needed that comfort of knowing my purpose. Knowing my future. Now, I had no idea. I had no care in the world of what the next day was going to bring. No thought as to where I was going to sleep or where my next meal was coming from. One of the most important things to me was now irrelevant. I was so lost and had so little control. I just....I hate it. I hate thinking back on it, wondering how lost and out of it I must have looked.

It was now seven days before Christmas. A wonderful family's holiday was about to be ruined.

Thanks to me.

109

Colorado

This part of the episode is the one I feel most guilty about. When I think back on these instances, this particular day is the one that always stands out the most. It has brought me to tears numerous times. It's just gut-wrenching to me. I've spent numerous sessions in therapy discussing this day, begging and pleading that I could just take it back. Sure I caused stress and anxiety for my mother and my family, but I didn't physically take anything from them or put them in harm's way, except for my grandfather of course. I didn't directly involve them with all of this stuff from a criminal standpoint.

I know this stuff caused my mother pain that I will probably never be able to comprehend. I can only imagine what she was going through during those ten days. Ten days of confusion. Ten days of not knowing where I was, or even who I was. I tend to believe that what I put her through wasn't as bad as it could have been simply because I know how strong of a woman she is. I'm not saying it didn't affect her in the least, because I know for sure it did in many ways. But what I did to this particular family was just awful. Beyond words. I took things from this family that are impossible to replace. I'll do my best to try and explain my terrible deeds.

While talking with my mother to get more details about all of these things, she informed me that while I was on the run she had been calling everyone she knew to try and find out any information on my whereabouts. She called family and friends, fellow church members, anyone she could think of who might know something. One particular phone call from my mother to someone from a previous church that we had attended yielded some troubling information. The man she called informed my mother that he hadn't seen me or knew of anything that was going on with me. But…..he had some bad news to share. He informed her that their house had been broken into and their car had been stolen. My mother's reply?

"Jeremy took your car."

Now let's stop right here for a moment so that all of you can place yourselves in my mother's position. Your son is missing. You know he's AWOL from the Army. You know he's stolen a car. He's acting in a way that he has never acted in his entire life. You've put up flyers around town in hopes of finding him. You're now calling everyone that you know in hopes of finding some tiny bit of information that may lead you to him. And during this particular phone call, you have to come to a terrible realization and admit to this man that your son most likely broke into his home and stole his car. It's so heartbreaking to me. I'm filled with such regret and sorrow every time I look back on these moments. I'm also filled with the fear that these moments will define my past, and my future.

That must have been such a terrible position I had put my mother in. I can't imagine what was going through her mind when she hung up the phone. She went to such lengths to find out some kind of information about me, to try and lessen her confusion, only to be given information that probably confused her more. The worry, the stress, the anxiety, the not knowing. To this day I'm ashamed of having put her through all of that. I can't imagine trying to go to bed not knowing where one of my sons is at. Unfortunately, thanks to me, she's had to live through that. She's had to lay there in the darkness with worry keeping her awake. The strength it must have taken to finally close her eyes and pray for any amount of sleep, I just can't imagine. Mom, I'm so sorry for the hurt I unknowingly caused you.

Fortunately, for all of us, this man was a family friend and a member of our previous church. Once it was confirmed that it was me who did all of this to him and his family, they declined to press charges. An admirable act of kindness that I will forever be grateful for. They knew the things I had done to them weren't me. They knew what kind of child I was at church. They saw me grow up from a young kid into my late teens. I played with his children. We had church gatherings at their home. They knew me and my family well. But at this point, everyone who knew me knew *I* wasn't well. They knew that for me to commit these crimes against them something terrible had to be wrong.

Something terrible was wrong. And it was getting worse. At this point, my bipolar symptoms were beyond the maximum level. This is where some things are just a blur to me when I try to go back and remember specific details. I was a zombie. There was no internal part of me left. Just my body. Flesh and bones. Inside was vacant. Cobwebs. Roaches. Dust. At that point, I had absolutely zero control over what I was doing. None. It is a terrible feeling. To think back on how I was just walking around in broad daylight committing these crimes without a second thought is so saddening. In the moment it wasn't sad. I wasn't capable of that emotion at that time. I wasn't capable of anything at that time. I had no control, over anything. I was most likely born with the seed of this disorder already implanted in my brain. Tragic events throughout life would act as miracle grow and the seed would slowly spread roots that would intertwine all over, creating an even more irregular chemical imbalance.

For me, this disorder didn't just appear one day and assume command of my life. It groomed me. It slowly manipulated me to trust the decisions it made for me. This plan of manipulation was years in the making, and the initiation of that plan was spread out over many months. The process was slow and precise. It was so slow that I never saw any aspect of the attack coming. Once the initial schemes were in place, the bombardment of mental power attacked me from every angle. Rounds of OCD were fired from tanks moving up from the south. Infantry brigades of depression attacked from the east. And to seize full control, an atomic bomb of bipolar was dropped from miles above. This strategic plan of mental manipulation worked to perfection. I was at its mercy. And so was anyone I came into contact with.

Initiate Christmas holiday theft in 3...2...

New York

As I type this sentence, it is April 24, 2023. I started this book three years ago. Three years and I've only written 21,600 words. That's how hard it is to look back on these instances and put them to paper. Many times I've opened up my computer only to get two sentences into a particular part of the story and become upset and disgusted with myself and put my computer away. These days I can look back at those moments and know that it wasn't me making those choices. But that confirmation doesn't take away how bad I feel for doing them. It hurts to know what I did to others. But it also hurts knowing how controlled I was by the disorder. Looking back I was so hypnotized and out of body. It's just really sad to think about what these disorders can do to you.

Not only does writing these things bring back painful emotions, but every sentence is a reminder that I have mental disorders. And I always will. I'm not right in the head. I can't think normally for myself as most people can. I have to have medication to function properly. Every time I grab this computer to add more to this story I'm reminded of my disorders and the terrible things I did and the people I hurt. You never forget about them, especially when they've caused so much harm to others, and yourself. But not as much harm as I caused to this particular family.

As previously mentioned, I needed money. I guess I was under the impression that I was going to be running for the rest of my life. I was going to be a career criminal. So I needed funding and lots of it. I could no longer use banks. At this point, I was on every bank teller's mind and was being sought after by many law enforcement agencies. Where could I go to get money? Who did I know that had money? Well, there's my grandfather, but I've already taken everything I can from him. Who else has money? Aha! I know who has money, and lots of it. A family friend and owner of a very profitable local business. Cha-ching! All I have to do is break into their home in the middle of the day, take a bunch of their stuff, walk out the door and be on my way.

Simple enough.

I went to church with this family for about five or six years. Everyone knew they were very well off. They lived in a nice neighborhood in a really nice home. They had nice cars and such. There had to be something of value in their residence. Without any kind of planning or a single thought as to how I was going to pull this off, the devil steered the car to the somewhat wealthy neighborhood of Foxwood in northeast Jacksonville. Right next to this particular home is a country club, golf course, and a neighborhood pool. Part of the parking lot for the country club was right between the club itself and their home. There was a gate that led from the driveway of their guest house to the country club parking lot.

Now remember, this is broad daylight. I'm in no way trying to hide what I am doing or putting any effort into trying to be sneaky with my actions. I didn't drive by a few times to scope the place out. I didn't park a ways away to monitor the house for a while before going in. I did none of that. Now I didn't walk right into the home either, but I was definitely not trying to not be seen. I drove right up and parked in the country club parking lot right next to the house as if I belonged there. Did I sit in the car to calculate the moves I was about to make? Of course not. This is the demon we're talking about here. He and I were a tag team of on-the-edge criminals. Calculations? Planning? Monitoring? Ha!

Without hesitation, I got out of the stolen Grand Prix and casually made my way into the guest house that was between the actual house and the country club parking lot. I have now committed trespassing and breaking and entering. That's two more charges. I think we're at seven now, maybe eight. I'm beginning to lose count. I didn't even look to see if anyone may have been home. The fact that someone might be there and may have seen me never crossed my mind. I had been in this part of the property a few times before. We used to play hide and seek in this guest house during church cookouts, so I knew the layout pretty well. I also knew there wasn't much in there that would benefit me financially, but I did a scan of the place just to be sure.

I probably spent five to ten minutes in the guest house. After coming up empty I decided to shoot for the house itself. I found a spot near the right rear corner of the guest house that provided a vantage point to the garage area and the left side of the house, which held the kitchen area. There was a vehicle in the carport, so the chance of someone being home was pretty high. Did that deter me at all? Of course not. After waiting for a few minutes and seeing no movement in the kitchen, I made my way across the driveway from the guest house and towards the carport door that led into the kitchen.

Did I look around to see if anyone saw me? No. Did I look through the windows to double-check if people were there or not? Nope. Did I knock? No, I did not. Did I slowly creep through the door so as to not make any noise? Again, no. I am so manic and out of touch with reality that I just walked right in as if I lived there. Anyone could have been standing in that kitchen, yet I busted in as if I had just worked a twelve-hour shift and had nothing on my mind but a cold beer. To my knowledge, four people lived there, and I knew all of them. A mother, father, and two daughters. And I just walked right in as if I were a part of their family. What would I have even said if I encountered any of them inside their own home that I had just broken into?

"Umm hi. Remember me? Nice to see you all again. Sooooo… I'm here to rob you."

Nevada

L uckily for me, and them, not a single person was home. I did not find this out by searching the entire home for someone. I found out later after all of this was over that no one was there. I broke into this home and didn't even bother searching the entire place to see if anyone was in it. I didn't even go upstairs. There could have been someone up there while I was rooting around this home looking for something to benefit me on my journey. Anyone could have walked around a corner and saw me. I wasn't peaking around corners or trying to be quiet with every move I made. I was just....there.

Imagine yourself in your own home looking for that one item you hardly ever use. You're just casually making your way through the house, oblivious to anything else going on around you. The only thing that's on your mind is finding the rubber bands. That's exactly how I was making my way through this home. I may as well have taken my shoes off and made myself comfortable as I walked about. I was so lost and out of mind that the possibility of anyone being there just didn't register with me. Every part of my mind was so governed and so focused on these rash decisions that I was incapable of thinking about the consequences of them. The best I can describe my speed and demeanor would be like I was walking around a museum. I patiently strolled through this house as if I had just paid twenty bucks to stare at abstract paintings that made no sense.

Once I was inside the kitchen I just stood there for a moment. My mind was racing so much that I had no clue what to do next now that I was in there. I think maybe I might have been shocked that I even made it that far without being caught. After looking around in the kitchen and dining room area I concluded there was nothing there that would help me so I strolled into the living room. The first thing I remember seeing upon entering the living room was the country club golf course through the back porch windows of the home. I continued scanning my evil eyes further around the living room and eventually noticed their Christmas tree to my left. And of course, under the tree were presents. Lots of them. Jackpot! Without hesitation, I grabbed as many as I could and took them to the kitchen and sat them on the floor next to the carport door. I can't recall how many and I don't even remember opening any of them. But I do know I stole quite a few Christmas presents from this family.

I've just committed theft. Again. What are we at? Nine felonies? Lord help me. I remember searching the kitchen trying to find a trash bag to put the gifts in. I didn't want these presents, I wanted the rush that came with stealing them. The mania needed to be constantly fed. It seemed the more I fed the mania, the more of a rush the mania needed. I took a trash bag full of gifts out to the carport and set them down on the steps that led into the kitchen. I'm now a modern-day Grinch. I went there for money and there I was taking presents I didn't even need. Still to this point, it had never occurred to me that anyone may have seen me or that anyone could pull up at any moment. What would I even do at that point? Run? I would find out during interrogation that their neighbors across the street had seen me arrive and leave. But because of the way I was acting, just being casual the entire time, they assumed it was okay that I was there. So no law enforcement was ever notified.

After depositing the bag of loot outside, I went back into the house and decided to make my way through the rest of the downstairs area. I remember winding through a couple of hallways and I think I passed through a formal dining room at the front of the house. There were trinkets and fancy decorations throughout, but nothing that could help me financially in its current form. I needed cash, some kind of legal tender. There had to be something in this house. And I would eventually find it. A hallway at the opposite end of the home from the kitchen led me towards the master bedroom. I remember searching through all of the bedside table drawers and a few dresser drawers. I think I may have taken some jewelry, I'm not 100% sure, but flashes of jewelry are in my memory of this moment. I know for a fact that I took a VCR tape that was sitting on their bedroom entertainment center. Why? I have absolutely no clue. How bizarre is that?! A freaking VCR tape!

Anyway, after stealing ridiculous things like VCR tapes, I made my way to the bathroom which was in the back right corner of the bedroom. Through the bathroom was the walk-in closet. And as I walked into the closet I immediately noticed a medium-sized safe on the floor.

"We've done it. Get it open so we can revel in our spoils. Now!"

Okay, okay. I'm on it.

I needed something to break it open, or, the code. That would be much easier of course. I checked the back of the safe to see if maybe a code had been written somewhere. I checked all over the closet for something that might contain the code. Nothing. But first, before I open this safe, I need to take the presents to the car. Why I stopped working on the safe to take the presents from the steps to the car I have no idea. But there I was, just casually walking across their driveway towards the Grand Prix with a bunch of stolen presents slung over my shoulder. However, the vehicle in the carport caught my eye. An early 2000's Ford Thunderbird was much nicer than what I was driving in. And let's face it, I needed a new ride because the Grand Prix was on every police officer's radar at this point. Sometimes your mind helps you out during a manic episode, but most of the time it doesn't. I walked back into the kitchen and found the keys to the Thunderbird hanging on the wall just inside the door.

I loaded the presents into the car and made my way back inside to work on the safe. It was too heavy to carry all the way to the car. I wasn't going to be able to take it with me and I didn't want to leave it without knowing what was inside. Curiosity was killing the cat. I had to get it open. My ticket out of my current situation could be inside. I went back to the kitchen and started looking around in the cabinets. After a few minutes of searching, I found the instruction manual to the safe. I flipped through a few pages of the book and to my surprise I saw four numbers written on the corner of one of the pages. Bingo! I ran to the closet with the manual in my hand and crouched down on one knee in front of the safe. Tap-tap-tap-tap. The anticipation I was feeling during those 'taps' provided as good of a high as any drug probably could. After I entered the four numbers I heard a click. My heart stopped. The bolt unlocked and I opened the door.

What I saw was beyond anything I could have ever imagined.

And it wasn't money.

Arizona

G old, gold, and more gold.

Jackpot!

Row after row of solid gold mint coins in plastic tubes. In addition to the gold coins were other collector coins of gold and silver. Some were in wooden cases and even had certificates of authenticity. It was a huge gold and rare coin collection. I think I took all of it, I may have left some collectors' boxes that were too big but I think I took the majority of it. I had never physically touched actual solid gold my entire life. My eyes were beaming at every tube of gold coin I pulled out and placed in the bag. I had still yet to pick up my pace. I sat there stunned and took the time to admire everything. I made a couple of trips to the Thunderbird with the coins. I now had what I needed. I was set for a long, long time.

The price per ounce of gold in 2002 closed the year on the stock market at around $347.00. If my memory serves me correctly, I had around 150-200 solid gold 1-ounce bullion coins. So just in gold coins alone, I had anywhere from $52,050-$69,400. Along with the other twenty or so collectible coins I had, I was probably in possession of around $100,000 worth of gold and coins altogether. How much did I get for these coins? Around $20,000. Why? Because I'm an idiot who had never held gold in my hand before and I went to a pawnshop to sell them.

After loading the car with everything, I realized I needed to get rid of the Grand Prix that was sitting in the parking lot next to the house. I couldn't leave it there. Every cop in the city was looking for that car. If I had left it there they'd see it when they came to investigate the breaking and entering. What to do, what to do…

"Go drive it up the block, walk back to the house, get in the Thunderbird and be on your way, you idiot."

More instructions forced into my head. More instructions immediately followed and obeyed. Now imagine if you will, I've just loaded this car with everything I've stolen, and now I'm going to drive the first stolen car a few blocks up the road and then casually walk back and get in the new car and leave. Did I mention casually? And in the middle of the day? This is insane! Looking back on this particular moment, if I had been thinking clearly, I probably would have driven the Thunderbird up the block first to get that part over with before someone came home. And then I would have come back and gotten the Grand Prix. But ninety-nine percent of the time you don't have the ability to think that way during a manic episode.

So I drove the Grand Prix up the street and over a hill. I grabbed my belongings and left the keys in the car. I then walked all the way back about three blocks to the newly stolen car. From me initially pulling up to the side of the house to rob it, to me walking back down the hill and getting into the new stolen car and leaving, was about thirty minutes. This was no quick smash-and-grab job. This was the complete opposite. This was casually move and slowly pick up. I methodically made my way through that house with absolutely no care in the world, because my disorder told me not to care. I had no clue what I was doing. I had no clue where I was.

I knew where I was from a directional and physical standpoint. I knew I was in Jacksonville, my old hometown. I knew I was in the home of a person I knew. But as far as being in the moment and knowing what I was doing and what mental and emotional state I was in, I had no clue where I was. I probably couldn't have told you my name if you walked up and introduced yourself to me. It hurts me so bad looking back and thinking of them pulling up to see their car gone. Then not knowing if it was even safe to walk into their own home. And then realizing that so many things had been taken. I just can't imagine how that must have felt.

Now that I had gone through this family's home, invaded their privacy, and ruined their entire Christmas holiday, it was time to hit the road and make my escape. I had stolen their presents. I had stolen their coins. I had robbed them of their sense of security and taken holiday memories. And in the car I had also stolen from them, I made my way out of the Foxwood neighborhood of Jacksonville Arkansas unscathed. Where I was headed now I had no clue.

But I knew it had to be far away from here.

Georgia

Where to go? Where to go? I wasn't quite sure, but I knew I needed to get on a freeway and out of the area, and quickly. I now had nine or so felonies and was still in the city where I committed eight of them. How about West? No, I definitely couldn't go that way. The Sierra Vista police and the military police were looking for me out that way. That would be a disaster of a plan. South? Well, I was pretty much already in the South. Not much further south I could have gone. North? I had never been that way in my entire life. I knew no one there and wouldn't have any idea where to go. So I stuck to an area I somewhat already knew. East.

"Yes, go east. No one will know where you are."

Okay. East it is.

Where East, I had no clue. I'd figure that out on the way. I just needed to get on the freeway and get the hell out of the area. The furthest East I remember being was Georgia for my Advanced Individual Training after Basic Training. But we weren't allowed to leave the base because we were still trainees, so I didn't know much about the area. I had been to Nashville a time or two but didn't know the place well enough to be comfortable while on the run. But, I had been in the Memphis area many times and definitely knew my way around, somewhat.

Eastbound! I-40, baby! I took the back way South from Jacksonville and hopped onto the interstate at the Remington Rd. interchange. On my way to the freeway, I came within 2 blocks of my mother's home. It never crossed my mind to stop. I don't think I could've stopped even if it did cross my mind. I was on mental cruise control. I was riding in style in another car I had just stolen that was filled with a bunch of gold and Christmas presents I had also stolen. The car wasn't mine. Nothing in it was mine. If I had been pulled over I would have gone straight to jail because my name was nowhere on any of the registration documents. To JAIL! Did that ever occur to me? Not a single time. It's now a few days into this ordeal and the thoughts of going to my mother's or turning myself in or getting help somewhere had yet to enter my mind. The rush I was experiencing was just too great. The mania made me feel like Superman. Finding the next thing to feed that mania and to keep the rush going were the only things on my mind.

In a sense, like in the movie 'The Matrix', this disorder downloads itself into your mind. It slowly takes over all of the RAM in your brain. In 'The Matrix' you could download anything into your mind. Anything. Need to know how to operate a helicopter? Zap! And you instantly knew how to do it. Need to know kung fu? Zap! And you instantly knew how to defend yourself with the martial arts. Zap!

And bipolar instantly has control over every aspect of your thoughts, your moods, and your decisions. It also controls your reactions to those thoughts, moods and decisions. You will steal this car and you will be happy doing it. Zap! You will steal irreplaceable holiday memories from a family. Zap!

It's so hard to explain to someone who has never experienced a bipolar episode exactly how lost and out of control bipolar makes you feel. Even in the rare instances where you realize that what you're doing is bipolar-related, you're powerless to stop it. Sometimes it even feels Stockholm Syndrome-esque. You're tricked into thinking that your disorder is right, about everything. I constantly find myself sitting in silence staring at this screen trying to type and explain what it feels like to be in a bipolar mania episode. And every time I keep coming back to 'a roller coaster ride'. What happens to you when you get on a roller coaster after you are strapped in? You are there FOR GOOD. When that bar comes down over your chest you no longer have control, of anything. In an instant, you go from having complete control of everything in your life to having no control over anything. You are at the mercy of the ride and the seventeen-year-old who's tapping buttons and controlling it while talking with her friends.

"Like, oh my God. Did you see Jennifer at the party last night? I know, right? She should *not* be wearing that. Ugh, hang on, let me turn on this roller coaster…."

Your control of everything is gone. Taken from you. And after you lose that control, you experience highs and lows at varying speeds. Some of those highs and lows you enjoy, some you don't. But you are forced to face those two things. You are forced into those two scenarios because all control has been stolen from you. You have no other options in life at that moment. You are along for the ride, literally. The two huge differences being that you *chose to* get on the ride and you can *choose* to get off of it once it's done. Those with bipolar don't get to make those two choices. You cannot stop a bipolar episode from starting, and you can't end it whenever you choose to. You are on that mental roller coaster, with absolutely no control, until it decides to stop.

If I had gotten pulled over at any point during this criminal trip, I would have been going to jail for a very long time. None of that worried me one bit. Bipolar hadn't permitted me to worry about that. I didn't have the ability to worry about any of the consequences. Sitting here and typing this sentence, I'm curious as to what I would have done had a cop tried to pull me over. I'm of the opinion that I probably would have hit the gas and tried to run. Simply because of the rush that it would have provided. Luckily that never happened. I made it out of Jacksonville unscathed, again. After a couple of hours into the drive, I was entering West Memphis. And before crossing the mighty Mississippi, I noticed a billboard for the Tunica casino resorts. Oh heck yeah! That's what I'm talking about! A quiet, small town out in the middle of nowhere where I can gamble away everything I had just stolen. A place where no one knows who I am. Most people want to go where they feel wanted, where they feel important. A place where everyone knows who they are.

Cue the 'Cheers' theme.

You sang it. Don't lie.

I wanted the opposite. I wanted away from everyone and everything I knew. I wanted away from myself. Which is probably the main thing that I kept running from.

Well, by this time, my partner in crime and I had put in a lot of work destroying other people's lives. It was now time to get us a room at the casino and live it up and try and relax.

The little devil and I did just that.

Arkansas

It's been a wild ride so far. Crime after crime. Felony after felony. A modern-day Clyde, with Bonnie on my shoulder. The more I write all of this out the more ashamed I become. I know it's been twenty years since all of this happened, but this is the first time I've actually sat in deep thought about these things. Sometimes something will happen that will remind me of doing this stuff and I'll just shake my head and usually go into a temporary depressive state. It may only last for a few hours but it hits hard. While writing the previous chapter, it occurred to me that I hadn't formally apologized to anyone that I stole from during this spree. I feel like I apologized to the mother and father with a letter but I'm not quite sure. Even if I did, I was probably not well mentally and the apology probably wasn't very sincere.

So I sat down and looked all of them up online and sent them all an apology. Apologies are hard. Describing feelings is hard, for most everyone. I had to sit down and write how sorry I was for not only stealing this family's personal items, but for stealing Christmas memories from them. For stealing their sense of safety, security, and comfort. I took time from this family. Instead of enjoying each other's company on

Christmas morning, they were probably thinking about the teenager they used to go to church with walking around in their home and going through all of their things.

The father responded the next morning and graciously accepted my apology, as I figured he would. That's just the kind of person he's always been. They are all such amazing and compassionate people. His acceptance made my entire world easier. It relieved so much anxiety and stress. A weight was lifted. I have no idea why I waited so long to apologize, but I'm glad I finally did it. It has truly helped in my healing process, and I hope it helped them as well.

Now, before my little evil pal and I could get a hotel room, I needed some cash. I had a fortune with me, but none of it was in spendable form. I crossed over the I-40 bridge into downtown Memphis and drove around until I found a pawnshop. This was before the days of having Google on your phone, so it's not like I could just do a search and GPS my way somewhere. I pulled into the parking lot of a nice-looking pawnshop and sat in the car for a while so I could conjure up a story as to where I got all of this gold from. It had to sound legit and reasonable. But let's face it, no matter what I said they were going to know it was stolen. How many twenty-four-year-olds are walking around with tubes of gold bullion and coins?

I came up with the best BS story I could, grabbed a tube from the back seat, worked up some courage and made my way into the store. The story I came up with was ridiculous, to say the least. But the guy in the pawnshop accepted it.

"Well, this is some mighty fine bullion you have here. Where did you get it if you don't mind me asking?"

"It's my grandfather's. He's become really disabled and it's gotten to the point where he's no longer able to get around and is now wheelchair-bound. So he's having to make some changes to his house so he can get around in his wheelchair and reach cabinets and stuff. He's not giving this to me. He just sent me to cash it in because he's not able to come here on his own really."

Pretty good story huh? No, it's a sick story. Not only had I already stolen from my Grandfather days before, but I was now using his likeness in a lie to try and sell something I had stolen from someone else. What the hell is wrong with me? I couldn't be more of a sad and pathetic excuse of a human if I tried. The evil lengths I was pushed to, it's just so sad for me to think about sometimes. Fortunately, the clerk thought it was a good enough lie, or he just really wanted the gold. He walked over to another clerk and showed him my product. The other clerk glanced over at me and then back to his associate. They talked a bit more and the clerk came back over to me and said, "You've got yourself a deal."

"We'll give you $10,000 for the tube you brought in. We can give you $2,000 in cash now and we'll write you a check for the remainder and you can cash it tomorrow. That'll be alright with ya?"

"Yes, sir. Sounds good."

In my mind I'm thinking, HECK YEAH! CHA-CHING! CHA-CHING!

He counted out two thousand dollars and placed it in my hand. I had never been in possession of that much cash in my entire life. I told him thanks and that I'd wait and cash the check in the afternoon the next day just to make sure their account could handle it. I pocketed my two grand and walked out the door. I jumped in the car and started yelling and laughing as loud as I could. The high at this moment is indescribable. It's almost as if nothing else in the world existed except for what was happening to me. This criminal stuff sure was easy. I should have been doing this long ago. I was getting pretty good at it. Err... my disorder was getting good at it.

Let's be honest for a moment, it was quite amazing that I had done all of these things and traveled so far and the closest I had come to being caught was at the second bank trying to forge a check. Getting away with all of that stuff and having not been caught up to that point is mind-boggling to me. At the time, I had no clue I was breaking the law. Laws didn't exist to me. Not in the sense that I didn't respect the law, but in the sense that I didn't have the mental ability to even know I was doing anything wrong.

I pulled out of the pawnshop parking lot and went and found the biggest and greasiest fast food meal I could find. I sat in the stolen car and ate my artery-clogging feast while surrounded by gold and other items that weren't mine. I felt like I was sitting on a throne, looking down upon everything I ruled. Once I was done I headed south out of Memphis towards the bright lights of Tunica. I had been there once before with my fiance when her godparents took us. It's only five or six medium-sized casinos, nothing too extravagant. I had loved the Horseshoe casino the last time I had visited so that's where we decided to set up shop. We've turned a lot of lives upside down.

Let's try and turn Tunica upside down as well.

Pennsylvania

Let's pause here for a moment and go over something I mentioned previously about this disorder. During a manic episode, especially one like I was going through, you have more adrenaline rushing through your body than you know what to do with. Imagine feeling like you never have to sleep. You never have to sit down and rest or take a short nap. You always have energy. Your eyes are never heavy. You are never tired at all. Ever. That jolt you get from your morning coffee? Well, imagine having that jolt every second of the day, and every second of the night. It's like having a superpower. There is nothing that you can't do. Your mind is filled with so many thoughts, and those thoughts act as fuel providing energy to your entire body. Any thought or idea that pops into your head has to be completed. Why? Because you have the energy to do so. To me, wasting that energy would make me a failure.

There is an action movie titled 'Crank' starring Jason Statham. In this movie, he wakes up to discover that he's been poisoned and only has hours to live. In order to stay alive to try and find a concoction to reverse the poison, he has to keep his adrenaline on full tilt. So he is doing everything he can to stay energized. He's beating people up. He's having sex in the middle of the street in front of everyone. Performing death-defying stuff just to keep his heart rate up to fight off the toxin. This is what a manic episode feels like. It is forced adrenaline every minute of the day until someone gets you help or the episode subsides on its own. The person going through the episode is rarely the one to recognize it and seek help.

I left Arizona on the 14th of December. It was now coming up on the evening of the 18th, and I had yet to sleep, at all. Almost five days non-stop. An adrenaline-filled crime rampage. Sleep was the last thing on my mind. I never thought of it. Looking back I don't think I ever felt tired at any point, ever. Sleep wasn't an option. I didn't have a say in the matter. There is no relaxation during a manic episode. You do one thing after the other. You feed off of the gratification of spending a bunch of money on something you don't need. Then you go and spend money on something else you'll never use. You're not buying the item. You're buying the rush. The thrill.

That feeling you get when you walk away from the register with something in your hand that wasn't yours five seconds ago, that's what you're buying. THAT'S why you bought it. The mania feeds off of that feeling and makes you want more of that feeling. It forces you to feed the mania by continuing to buy stuff. By making rash decisions. The disorder and the episode it has created force you into thinking that you need that rush to survive. That rush feels so good, too. You feel on top of the world. There is nothing you can't do. And nothing you won't do. It's so painful to look back on. I try to picture myself in all of these scenarios, not having a clue what was happening and not having any say in what was going on.

I tend to speak more about the manic states of bipolar more than I do the depressive states. I have had some depressive states in my life due to bipolar but not many. My depressive episodes are very short, maybe two to three days, and maybe two to three times a year. Though rare, they are strong and come on with full force. And they come on instantly. One minute I'll be happy and doing something I enjoy. The next minute I will be saddened and overcome with emotion wondering if the bug my cat just ate had a fulfilling life before going through such a horrific death. I will become saddened by that bug's fate and I will sit and contemplate life for the next thirty minutes. My brain is wired to do that kind of crazy stuff.

Worse than surrendering control of your mind during those moments, is how much of your life those moments take from you. I mean, instead of doing something with my boys I'm on the couch contemplating the life of a bug, and the fact that my cat doesn't give a damn about what just happened. Mania, OCD, and depression, they're all difficult to deal with. They're even harder to deal with when you realize how much time they take away from your life.

Like most, I'm usually pretty quiet during my depressive phases. I embarrass myself with some of my actions. I become sad when I can't do normal, everyday things. The depressive episode will make me think I'm a failure because I forgot to hit the 'start' button after setting the timer on the dryer an hour ago. Normally I would just laugh it off or even post on Facebook how forgetful I am sometimes. But in a bipolar depressive state, setting the timer but forgetting to hit the start button is devastating to me. It destroys my character. It affects my mentality for the rest of that day. It makes me feel like I'm a failure. It makes me question everything. Luckily my depression doesn't affect me as much. My mania is much better these days but it still gives me fits more than the depression does.

It's 9:30 p.m., Sunday, August 20th, 2023, and my 'depakote pill' alarm just went off on my phone. Oh, how I despise that alarm. How I despise these pills.

What I despise even more is the fact that I need them to survive.

Virginia

I now had two thousand dollars of someone else's money burning a hole in my pocket, minus what I spent on that huge, greasy meal of course. I walked into the Horseshoe Casino like I owned the place. Like I hadn't just stolen a car and driven all the way from Arizona and forged my own Grandfather's checks and stolen a second car from someone else. In my mind, I hadn't done any of that stuff. The only thing that ever mattered to me was what was happening at that very moment. If it wasn't happening 'right then', then it never happened. I was forced to live one second at a time. What happened the previous second was none of my business. It was irrelevant to me.

It was time to get a room, have some fun, and relax. Instead of paying much less and getting a hotel room in town and driving back and forth to the casino, I decided to spend lots of extra cash and spring for a room at the Horseshoe Casino. The cost of the room itself is where most of my money went. But I didn't care. Remember, I didn't have the ability to care. They could have told me any ridiculous price for the room and I would have paid it. I don't recall how much it was, but I know it wasn't cheap. But what the hell? I had money. And I had eight thousand more coming the next day. Finances were no longer a problem for me. I unloaded what I needed from the car and made my way up to my room. Did I choose to relax and maybe get some sleep? Of course not. I, I mean my mind, chose to have some fun. After throwing everything on the bed I immediately hit the casino floor. My rush had not been fulfilled yet. I needed more of that feeling. I was addicted to that feeling. According to me, that rush was the only thing keeping me alive.

I made my way back down to the lobby and stepped out of the elevator like I was Robert De Niro in 'Casino'. This place was now mine. I lit a cig and casually strolled around all of the games designed to take my money. I soaked in the sights and sounds, the flashing lights of hope all around. I was so high on mania that it felt like my feet weren't even touching the floor. Like I was an Egyptian god being carried around in a chair. After a bit of perusing, I found my favorite spot. The five-dollar blackjack table. I laid down two hundred to hold my spot until the next hand was dealt. I lit up another cigarette and listened to the band performing in the corner by the bar. There I sat, in the bright, captivating lights of the lobby of the Horseshoe Casino. A felon. Everyone around me was most likely a law-abiding citizen and not running from the law. They all probably had a home they would go to once their luck ran out. I had no place to go to. And even if I did my demon probably wouldn't allow it. At this point, wherever I was at was my home.

"Changing two hundred! the dealer shouted to the pit boss.

"Two Hundred!", he shouted back.

"Would you like nickels, dimes, or quarters?"

"Nickels please."

Just FYI, that's casino lingo. 'Quarters' refers to a $25 chip and 'nickel' is referring to a $5 chip. This being a $5 table I decided to start with the lowest denominator. I like to play more hands at a lower cost than fewer hands at a high cost. The atmosphere and entertainment are more important to me than the winning. I did okay at the table for not having played in so long, and for my mind being totally wired. I'm surprised I was even able to slow down my mind enough to understand and remember the rules of the game. Surprisingly, I walked away from the table up a few hundred dollars. I had run out of cigarettes and wasn't going to pay the outrageous prices the casinos charged when I had my own smokes up in my room.

I think this was when I slept for the first time since leaving Arizona, almost five days earlier. I guess the rush I got from winning at a blackjack table was enough of a rush to calm my mania and allow me to be able to get a bit of sleep. As far as I can remember, this would be the only night I would sleep. In a matter of ten days, I probably slept a total of 12 hours. I probably looked it, but I sure as heck didn't feel it. I felt amazing. The next day I drove back to downtown Memphis to cash the check the pawnshop had given me. While I was in the area I decided to stop back by the shop to see if they wanted any more of my loot. I walked out of the store with another two thousand in cash for a second tube of coins, and a second check for another eight thousand dollars for the remainder of the second transaction.

Max rush. We've hit max rush!

I went to such illegal extremes to get all of this money, yet I had no idea what to do with it now that I had it. Am I going to be on the run for the rest of my life? Do I need to hold on to some of this money to live? Where does one keep almost twenty thousand dollars while on the run? During that time, none of that worried me. I thought of none of that. I was one hundred percent in the moment. The next minute of my life was miles away. How my current actions would affect my future never crossed my mind. I wasn't able to decipher my current actions. They weren't even my actions. At this point in the manic episode, I am nothing more than the Tin Man, walking around with an empty shell of a body.

Any movement I made, any word I said, any thought that entered or left my mind was all controlled by my disorder. As I'm writing this, it's been twenty years since all of this happened. Even a year after it happened some of the episode was a blur. I only remember bits and pieces, thankfully. I think if I were able to remember all of the details of everything I did it would take me even longer to heal.

I'm satisfied not knowing and remembering everything.

Washington

I now had more money than I knew what to do with. I was living in a casino. And I was in the midst of the worst bipolar manic episode in the history of history. Not a great combination. For the next few days, I would hide out in the casino. Not that I was *trying* to hide. I mean I gave them my actual name when I checked in. On some level, I think I may have been trying to steer clear of the authorities. Yet on another level, I think I hoped that I was caught so I could get help. Some days were spent in my room, curled up in a ball of confusion. Some were spent wandering around the casino floor jumping from slot machine to slot machine. This was back when slot machines actually paid out tokens that you had to cash in. I'd lose money, I'd make money. I'd try to sleep. Lose more money, make more money. I would call my mother and quote bible verses to her and then hang up before she even had a chance to reply. I have no idea why I did that. Looking back I think it was to let her know I was still alive. Not okay, but alive.

I've called my mother numerous times to get the correct information to help me write a lot of this book. She relayed to me that my dealings with the pawnshop were what got the authorities closing in on my trail. She didn't remember the specifics of the investigation, but apparently, the pawnshop owners contacted the authorities. So that means a day or two after cashing the second check, while I was living in the casino, the Memphis authorities were on to me.

I had now been at the casino for five days and I was on the run in a very noticeable and rare car. And the Memphis police were now looking for me. I was doing all of my traveling in an early 2000s bright red Ford Thunderbird convertible. Hello! There couldn't have been but a handful of those around that area at the time. How I made it so long without getting caught has always made me question the authorities who were looking for me.

I found the nearest branch of the bank the pawnshop used and cashed the second eight-thousand dollar check. I went back to the casino to gamble my life away. Now, I will not hesitate to tell anyone how bad at math I am. I know the basics and can do some good math in my head. But statistics and percentages and such have always eluded me. Put me in a math failing competition and I will win every time. I was just never able to grasp the concepts. On paper, yes. In my mind on my own, no, it's not happening. That being said, while at the blackjack table one evening, somehow I was able to run a couple hundred dollars up into the thousands in about eight hours. Yes, thousands. They actually tried to move me to a different table with larger denominations but I refused.

I specifically remember this moment because others at the table would continuously ask me how much I started with and how long I had been at the table. Now remember, I'm terrible at math, so there is absolutely no way in hell I'm counting cards. It's just not happening. I am under the impression that the mania is what led me to make the decisions I did that increased my odds of winning. I was hitting on cards that you're not usually supposed to hit on. I had a huge stack of chips that hours ago was just a few five-dollar chips. I remember asking the dealer to count my chips so I could go use the restroom. She looked at me and said twelve thousand.

I had been at the table most of that evening. I was growing weary and needed a break. But my mania hadn't gotten the rush that it needed to survive. I was at its beck and call. I would eventually drive up my total to around fifteen thousand dollars. I had now drawn a crowd, which wasn't good. The crowd agitated me. They made me nervous. I was now under pressure to perform. I was giving waitresses twenty-five dollar chips for bringing me drinks. We were high-fiving each other for every hand won. The dealer was shaking her head, she had never witnessed such a run by a player. I was so in a zone. I couldn't bust if I tried. A person being in a normal mood and normal mental state would be cautious to 'hit' on 15. Given the mental state I was in I was definitely not being cautious. I wasn't paying for each hand, I was paying for the anticipation that came with the flip of each card. And it was paying off. Each flip fed the rush. And each flip demanded more of that rush. It was a sickening cycle.

I was doing so well for so long that the pit boss came over and closed the table to change out the chute because they were under the impression that I was counting cards. Recognizing his move, I made a move of my own. I grabbed my money and cashed out. I had already been at the table the entire evening. And apparently, the little guy in control of my mind had gotten the rush he needed. I remember leaving the table and going to one of the restaurants and ordering a huge steak dinner. It was probably the only full-course meal I had had in 9 days.

This was the evening of December 23rd, 2002. In less than twenty-four hours I would be in another psychiatric institution.

Delaware

Do you remember what you were doing on December 24th, 2002? You were probably preparing for Christmas morning. Maybe you were in the kitchen getting a nice holiday meal ready. You might have been at a Christmas church service. You may have even been finishing up last-minute shopping and wrapping presents.

I remember exactly where I was. I was sitting at the end of a bed in the Horseshoe Casino of Tunica, MS, descending rapidly from an insane bipolar manic episode. I was at the end of the roller coaster ride. I had just gone through the last turn at blazing speed and had come to an immediate screeching halt. It was all over. Just like that. The stealing, burglarizing, and running had finally come to an end. The demon had been satisfied. It had been triumphant in ruining my life and the lives of others. It crawled back into its hiding place far into the depths of my cerebral matter. It wouldn't come back around for many years.

While you were high on Christmas cheer, I was hiding what remained of the stolen cash underneath a dumpster in the parking deck of the casino. That's right. All of the remaining money was thrown under a dumpster. Why, I have no idea. So no one else could spend it I guess. Or maybe so I wouldn't get caught with it. I have no clue. All I remember is walking out of the casino with a few personal items and one thing on my mind, getting to my mother. And I couldn't get there fast enough.

My mania subsided enough to the point that I was able to realize that something was seriously wrong. What that was I had no idea. But at that moment, an extreme desire for help had taken over my entire body. I knew I needed immediate assistance, I just didn't know what for. I had no idea what I had done in the last few days and no idea who I had hurt. The insane criminal escapade was over. There was nothing left but a trail of destruction across six states with bits and pieces of my mind scattered about. In a matter of ten days, I had destroyed my life and the lives of my family and others.

I was AWOL from the Army. I had numerous theft, forgery, and burglary felonies racked up. Plus two counts of grand theft auto and theft of mail, which in itself is a federal offense. One of the nights while I was staying in Tunica, I drove around the local neighborhoods stealing people's mail. I guess because it was nearing Christmas and people were probably getting money and gift cards. I don't remember opening a single piece. The rush of stealing it was probably all I was needing at the time.

After loading my things in the car and disposing of the money, I drove out of the casino parking lot and headed back home to Jacksonville, AR. Every single bit of cash I had was now under a dumpster. I had to steal a tank of gas to be able to finish the trip home. Back in those days, you could actually pump your gas without prepaying. And given the car I was in I'm sure they weren't too worried about me stealing anything. A slant smile and wave to the cashier and he turned the pump on for me. A full tank of gas later and I was gone and back on the freeway.

Two hours later I would arrive at my mother's house. I never called her to let her know I was on the way. I simply showed up. I remember parking the car around the back of the house. I don't remember much of the arrival. I feel like someone met me on the porch, but I can't recall who it was. There was no anger towards me. No yelling or belittling. I didn't say much. All I remember is walking in and sitting on the couch. I felt so confused but extremely relaxed. I think I remember my older brother going outside to secure the car. A car that was filled with gold coins, mail, and presents.

There were so many things running through my mind at the time. What all happened? How much trouble was I in? What is wrong with me? Did I just do all of these things that they're telling me I did? Why did everything stop all of a sudden? It was the most confused state of mind I had ever experienced. I still felt like I was being controlled by puppet strings. Completely disoriented. I don't know what all happened once I showed up at my mother's house. I don't even remember the ride to the hospital. From her house to the VA hospital is about a forty-minute drive. I remember none of it. I don't even recall who was driving or if anyone else was in the car.

No one called the police. My family wanted to make sure I got help first. They knew something was wrong with me. Everyone knew. Consequences for my actions would be faced later, but my mother wanted to do her best to make sure I got as much treatment as possible before going to jail. Myself still legally in the military, she took me to the emergency room of John L. McClellan Veteran's Hospital in Little Rock. I don't know what all was communicated to the staff about my situation. All I remember is sitting in the ER waiting room like a zombie. I don't recall anything about being in an actual ER room where they did the blood work and everything. I have no recollection of that. I only remember being in the waiting area.

My memory of all of this is just bits and pieces. It's like when you wake up from a dream and you have to hurry and tell someone about it because it was so crazy. After you tell them everything that you remember from the dream they give you a weird look and ask, "Then what happened?" And you have absolutely no clue! All you remember are small chunks that make absolutely no sense. This is my memory of my manic episode. Chunks. Bits and pieces.

One thing I do remember is a nurse telling either me or my mother that all drug tests came back negative. My mother probably already knew they would. I think it was just assurance on her part, so she would know what she was dealing with. I was discussing this book with my stepfather the other day and he had mentioned that he met us there at the emergency room. To this day I don't remember him being there at all. But I do remember that my next stop was the

3K Psych Ward at the Fort Roots VA Hospital in North Little Rock. I was sent there I suppose because of my actions and also because my mother had passed along to the medical staff that suicide ran in the family. I'm pretty sure she wanted eyes on me as much as possible.

I had turned myself in many hours ago and had yet to be incarcerated. Was I really going to dodge jail time and just have to rehabilitate in a psych ward?

Haha! Hell no. You're going to jail, bud!

Michigan

We all have those moments where we stop ourselves in our tracks and ask ourselves, 'What the hell am I doing with my life?' It could be in the middle of dinner. It could be while you're stuck in traffic. It could be when you get your paycheck and you notice all of the taxes taken from it. You could ponder your purpose anywhere, at any time. And you've probably done it many times. Many people go their whole lives never even getting in the vicinity of their purpose. Some people don't even care about finding their purpose. Does every person even have a purpose? What exactly *is* purpose?

Hey, Google!

pur·pose
   the reason for which something is done or created or for which something exists.

So, what is *your* purpose? Let's rephrase that question using a key word from the above definition.

Why do you exist?

Yikes! Hits a little harder when you put it like that, huh? What are you here for? What were you put here to do? What is your reason? Most Christians believe they were put here to serve the Lord. To follow and love him and spread the word of his love and sacrifice. Others believe that we are here simply to exist due to the result of two people who had sex. A lot of people just go with the flow throughout life and whatever they end up doing they just assume is their purpose, whether that be a plumber, lawyer, mechanic, secretary, mayor, or whatever. Growing up as a kid you might have wanted to be a police officer. Maybe you wanted to be a train operator. Or a race car driver. Is that how things turned out for you? Well, I hope so. But the majority of the time it doesn't.

Maybe even after high school you still had no clue what you wanted to do with your life. So you went to college and chose a degree in business management. Because well, everyone wants to manage a business or run their own business. Or you might have chosen something in the medical field because you're compassionate and like taking care of others. Maybe those paths didn't work out. Maybe you chose a path that was available and convenient at the time. Maybe your purpose ended up being something you never thought of, like mine. For some reason, we, especially me, engrain in our minds that our careers are our purpose. And sometimes that's true. But other things can be your purpose.

From about the tenth grade on, I had an inkling to be in the military. I went to basic training and AIT and then spent two years in the National Guard. I spent those two years working odd jobs and trying to figure out my purpose and what I wanted to be. I never figured it out so I went active duty Army. I soon found my purpose. I sunk my roots deep down into the Army. The connection was so right. I thrived. I woke up every day with purpose. With reason. This was what I was going to do for the rest of my life. I was content.

Sometimes we go for so long, and live so many years according to what we think we're supposed to be doing, only to find out we were put on this Earth to do something completely different. Twenty-five years ago I was one hundred percent positive that my purpose was to serve our country. Today I can confidently say that it wasn't. Do I now know my purpose? Yes, I do. Am I going to tell you right now? No, I'm not.

Ha!

Don't worry, you'll find out.

What I thought was my purpose was taken away. Quickly. Now I had to start all over to figure it out. But first I had to go through my second psych ward stint, followed up by some time in jail. It was inevitable. While at the 3K Psych Ward, I had no idea what was to come of my fate. I had no idea what was going on on the outside. No idea what my mother and family were doing to help me. I knew they were doing something, I just didn't know what. The 3K Psych Ward was very different than the ward at Fort Bliss, TX. We were free to roam the floor all day. They offered group therapy classes, had a small TV area, and offered reading and activity materials and such. It wasn't as strict as Fort Bliss. To me, it seemed like it was more of a place for patients to be monitored as they came down from whatever they were going through. It was a very helpful place, just in a different way.

I don't recall how many days I spent at 3K, but it wasn't long. I want to say about two weeks, maybe less. Once I was back on medications and seemed level-headed enough, I was sent to the Jacksonville, AR city jail, since Jacksonville is where most of my crimes were committed. The detective assigned to my case did not care one bit that I was bipolar or that I never had any run-ins with the law. Ever.

"Is this you?" he'd ask over and over while pointing to numerous surveillance photos of me inside the main branch of First Arkansas Bank & Trust waiting for a forged check to be cashed. "Is this you?" after pointing to a photo of me in the drive-thru lane at the other smaller bank branch.

"Son we have you on two forgeries, commercial burglary, and theft of property. And that's just charges in my jurisdiction. You're also AWOL from the Army, have a grand theft auto charge out of Arizona, and federal marshals are looking for you for stealing mail. Do you have any idea how long you're going to jail for? Anything to say? Is this you in these photos? Are you going to confirm or deny anything?"

Keep in mind I hadn't been read any rights. Hadn't been offered a phone call. Hadn't been offered to speak with a lawyer. Had no clue if this man had spoken with my family already. It was my second time ever in jail and going through any type of interrogation. Plus, I was still really messed up from what had just transpired. So it's not like I could wrap my mind around what all was going on and how to properly deal with everything from a judicial standpoint. I had no idea what to say to this prick. So I said absolutely nothing. Not a single word. I sat in silence. I didn't answer a single question. I didn't acknowledge anything he put in front of me. Once he figured out that I wasn't going to cooperate he gave up and sent me back to my cell.

Unfortunately, I was picked up from the 3K Psych Ward towards the end of the week. Which meant I had to sit in the Jacksonville city jail over the weekend to wait and see the judge the following Monday. It wasn't all bad. We were fed McDonald's every meal. The only bad part was that there were only two large cells and about ten people per cell. What was I going to say to the judge? It's not like I could deny any of it. There's proof of it all. There was only one thing I could say. How I knew of it I have no recollection. I probably got the idea from a TV show or a movie.

"Mr. Hughes. You have been charged by the state of Arkansas on two counts of forgery and one count each of commercial burglary and theft of property. How do you wish to plea?"

"Not guilty due to mental disorder or defect, your Honor."

"As you wish, Mr. Hughes. You will be sent to the Pulaski County Jail until proper court proceedings can be carried out. Next!"

County jail. Thank God. Although state prison was most likely in my future. I had no clue at this point. But county jail was much better than prison, that I knew. I was scared out of my mind, and it showed. Another inmate waiting for transport to county jail sat down with me and told me what to expect and to walk in with my head high and chest out. Anything less and you're toast.

Thanks for making me even more scared, dude.

My charges carried a minimum of eight years. If the family whose house I had broken into had chosen to press charges for stealing the gold and the car then it would have been even longer.

Figuring out my new purpose in life would have to wait. How long that wait would be, who knows? But I would soon have lots of time to think about it.

Docket Report Results PRODUCTION

Violations

HUGHES, JEREMY S

Violation: 1 Citation#: Age at Violation: 24 Plea: 14-APR-03 NOT GUILTY
5-37-201 FORGERY; FC Disp:14-APR-03 NOT GUILTY (ACQUITTAL)
Level: FC CLASS C FELONY
Violation Date: 16-DEC-02
Violation Time:

HUGHES, JEREMY S

Violation: 2 Citation#: Age at Violation: 24 Plea: 14-APR-03 NOT GUILTY
5-37-201 FORGERY; FC Disp:14-APR-03 NOT GUILTY (ACQUITTAL)
Level: FC CLASS C FELONY
Violation Date: 16-DEC-02
Violation Time:

Docket Report Results
PRODUCTION

Violations

HUGHES, JEREMY S

Violation: 1   **Citation#:**   **Age at Violation:** 24   **Plea:** 14-APR-03   NOT GUILTY
5-39-201   **BURGLARY COMMERCIAL; FB**   Disp:14-APR-03   NOT GUILTY (ACQUITTAL)
Level: FB   CLASS B FELONY
Violation Date: 19-DEC-02
Violation Time:

HUGHES, JEREMY S

Violation: 2   **Citation#:**   **Age at Violation:** 24   **Plea:** 14-APR-03   NOT GUILTY
5-36-103   **THEFT OF PROPERTY; FB**   Disp:14-APR-03   NOT GUILTY (ACQUITTAL)
Level: FB   CLASS B FELONY
Violation Date: 19-DEC-02
Violation Time:

Utah

Not long ago, I was prospering in the military. Serving my country. Advancing up the ranks. Fulfilling what I thought to be my purpose in life. Ten minutes into my arrival at the Pulaski County Jail I was stripped naked and being searched and then sprayed with a water hose. Yes, what you see in the movies is true, that part I can attest to. The in-processing at the county jail didn't take long. From the time I got there to the time I walked into my cell was probably about an hour. During that hour I had already concluded that my life was now over. Even when I got out of there who was going to hire me for any reputable job? Hardly anyone. My record would be filled with all kinds of extreme charges. One glance at my resume and the human resource officer is lying to my face about not having any positions open and is tossing it in the trash as soon as I walk out the door.

I couldn't worry about all of that right now. I needed to focus. I needed to initiate and manage my presence and persona in county jail. You hear horror stories about being in county jails and state prisons. I'm sure they differ from place to place. But honestly, and surprisingly, this was a cakewalk. As long as you weren't sent to our cell block on rape, child molestation, or child pornography charges, you were okay. I never had an issue with anyone. It was a well-run unit. Most inmates did what they were told. There were no sexual assaults in the showers or threats of physical harm or groups or gangs. It was nothing like that. You woke up. Ate breakfast. Read a book or watched TV in the day room. You could even go outside in the courtyard and light up a hand-rolled cigarette or play basketball on a 13-foot rim. All of the rims were raised so they couldn't be used as an escape route. The courtyard had a fenced top anyway. You weren't going anywhere even if you did manage to get on the basketball goal.

One night while some of us were watching the evening news, a report about a local child molester came on the TV. I don't remember what the man did, but I do know it was physical and that it involved numerous children. The next morning that same worthless pile of garbage was sent to our unit. We all immediately recognized his face from the TV report the night before. The first thing your cellmate asks you when you come on the unit is, "What are you in for"? You have two options. Lie, and get rid of your court documents so he can't find them. Or tell the truth and face the consequences. Unfortunately for this guy, we already knew what he had done. I had already told myself I wouldn't get involved with anything that might affect my record negatively unless it was self-defense. So I wasn't going to be interacting with this tool unless he did something to me.

It's one thing to get charged for child molestation. It's another thing to get charged for that and then continue with your same sexual ideations once you get to jail. All of our shower stalls were located in a corner along the second-floor catwalk. There was ONE spot in the entire unit where one could look up from a certain angle from the first floor and see into the shower stalls on the second floor. This idiot found that one spot his first day on the unit. The next day he had a black eye and crooked nose. This was the only physical confrontation that ever happened while I was there, that I knew of.

There are two things that you have a lot of in jail. Over-starched food and time. I probably gained twenty pounds while in county jail, which my frame had needed for years. I had always been tall and thin. I put on some extra weight due to physical activity in the Army but my metabolism was so high it was almost impossible to keep the weight on. Now, at forty-five, it's impossible to keep it off. I spent most of my time in jail thinking and playing basketball. There were many times when I would get a knock on my cell door followed by a shout of "Ski-J!", short for skinny Jeremy. Everyone in county gets a nickname, whether you want one or not.

"Yo, we need another one for basketball!" They had recognized my abilities and wanted me on their teams. I always jumped at the chance. It kept me occupied. It made the time go by, until what I had no idea. I was either getting everything dropped and going home or I was going to prison for a long time. County I could handle. Prison? ………nah.

Having so much time to just sit and think is great. But in my situation, having just gotten over a huge manic episode and capable of having another at any moment, having so much time to think was not a great thing. I needed to keep my mind busy. It felt like my mind would wander off out of control and I would have to really focus in on something to regain control. I tried not to think about going to prison, but I did every day. I thought about a lot of things while in jail. Life. My decisions throughout life. My childhood. Fishing with my dad. Wishing I had some of my mom's meatloaf instead of whatever it was that passed for meatloaf in that place. I wondered what my mother and brothers and sister were doing. How the family that I stole from was doing. How my grandfather handled everything. If any of them had forgiven me. How long I was going to be in there. If I was going to have another episode while incarcerated. And if I did would they be able to properly treat me.

I remember talking to my mother one day about getting out on bond. At the time it would have really put a lot of people in financial hardship to bail me out until court. The amount was set at $53,000. It just seemed more reasonable to wait it out. I didn't want to cause any more stress on anyone than I already had. So I toughed it out. Although I'm not sure 'tough' would be the proper word. My mother made sure I always had money in my account. There wasn't a day that went by where I didn't have snacks or stamps, or a day where I didn't get the newspaper. I was pretty popular on the unit. I made a lot of trades with the newspaper articles after I had read them. My mother always took care of me, no matter what situation I was in. So we agreed over the phone call, just sit in jail and wait for what would hopefully be good news from the attorney. Mom assured me that everything that could be done to try and get me out or to try and get me a light sentencing was being done.

I would soon find out where I would be going. Leaving this place was great news. Thankfully I wasn't going to prison.

But I wasn't going home either.

South Dakota

Almost three months into my time at the county jail, an officer approached my cell and informed me that later that afternoon I had an appointment with my attorney. I had already seen the attorney's a couple of times since I had been there. Honestly, I had absolutely no clue what they said either time. I left each meeting more confused than when I went in. Attorneys always talk in judicial lingo even when not in a courtroom atmosphere. They act as if everyone understands all those legal terms and such. A phone call with Mom always made everything less confusing. I usually contacted her a couple of times a week and after every meeting with the attorney or mental health doctor. Jail wasn't great, but I will say that they did stay on track with my mental situation. I saw a doctor a few times and got my bipolar medications daily.

This particular meeting with my attorney was not confusing at all.

"Mr. Hughes, we have presented to the prosecuting attorney a plan that doesn't involve prison time or even more time here, and you'll be happy to know that they have accepted it. I'm just here to run the deal by you so you understand all of what will be happening at your next court appearance."

"Wow. Well, that sounds great. What exactly *will* happen?"

"Well, your mother has put together a great case on your behalf with help from family members and friends. That, along with your clean criminal history and your recent bipolar diagnosis will be getting you out of any jail or prison time. However...."

Here it comes...

"You will be sent to the Arkansas State Hospital for sixty days. Upon proper completion of those sixty days, given that you don't have any issues during that time, you will be released on your own recognizance and entered into what is called the Arkansas Act 911 program for five years. The Act 911 program is a probation program for patients from the state hospital. You'll have to see an Act 911 representative each month. You'll have random drug testing. You will be enrolled into outpatient mental behavioral treatments at a facility we assign and you must attend monthly appointments."

Thanks to mental disorders, I had lost my purpose in the military, lost my reason for my existence, committed numerous criminal acts, and landed myself in jail. Thanks to mental disorders, I was now leaving jail.

Sadly, I do not remember my mother visiting me at all. Neither in the 3K Psych Ward nor while in the county jail. She has assured me that she visited many times, and I of course believe her. But it's so sad to me because there is something that's blocking out those memories of her being there. I have no recollection at all. I actually texted her during this paragraph to discuss her coming and visiting me at the hospital and the county jail. Not only did she help me tremendously during all of that, but she has helped a great deal in helping me remember things for this story. I do remember my younger brother coming to visit one or two times. He also came to visit me while at the VA 3K Psych Ward. Now being a parent myself, I can understand the emotional and mental toll all of this must have put on my mother. The book she put together showing what I had accomplished in the military and which also included letters from family and friends no doubt had an effect on my release. She was amazing. But seeing me in those situations I know took a toll on her.

The first time I *remember* seeing my mother since arriving at her house on Christmas Eve would be in Pulaski County Court. I could see her eyes begin to water as soon as we made eye contact. I was shackled and chained to people that had committed horrendous things. Drug dealers, rapists, and murderers. I was bound to these so-called people. Wherever they went, I had to follow. The thought of my mother seeing me like that killed me. I am ashamed of it to this day. Once seated we were unlocked from each other so we could come forward when our case was called. Many minutes and many cases would go by and I had yet to see my attorney anywhere. Twenty minutes later she was still nowhere to be found. What happens if my name is called and my attorney isn't here? I guess I go back to county and get rescheduled for another day.

Please don't do that to me. Just show up, *please*.

A few minutes before my name was called she busted through the doors. She immediately walked up to someone up front and handed them a bunch of paperwork while the judge and other attorneys were talking over a different case. My name was called next. I rose and made my way to the podium. She met me there, turned to me, and politely but sternly said, "Don't say a word". Whatever paperwork she handed to the person up front was already in the judge's hands. Everything had already been signed by the prosecutor and everyone had agreed on going to the state hospital and then enter the Act 911 program. Words were said, and assurances were made. A bunch of judicial lingo mumbo jumbo was yelled back and forth across the courtroom.

The judge shuffled through some paperwork and handed it to a clerk.

"Case dismissed."

My time in jail was now over.

A new beginning was about to begin.

Again.

(The book my mother put together that saved my life.)

To Whom It Concerns,

I have known Jeremy Hughes for almost his entire life. He and his family were members of the church I pastored in Monticello, Arkansas so I knew him in his formative years and was quite familiar with his family. In later years by chance his family also participated in the church I serve as pastor in Sherwood, Arkansas. I worked with him in our Youth Group and accompanied him and others on many outings. I ministered to his family in times of tragedy and trial such as his parents' divorce and the suicide of his older brother and later his own father.

Jeremy had what seemed a very normal childhood and adolescence. He was exemplary in his conduct with the occasional youthful indiscretion that is typical of teenage behavior. He was one of the kids I always called on for help when it was needed and he always responded positively. He was very dependable and always polite. This same outstanding behavior marked his character all the way through his early adulthood and most of his career in military service. Suddenly, and unexpectedly, he apparently was overtaken by some inner struggles that led to what can only be described as bizarre and uncharacteristic negative behavior. Being separated from a support system of family and friends played a role in this as did misdiagnosed and poorly treated mental health problems. No doubt he was very troubled by his parents' divorce and his father's suicide. No doubt the failure to resolve these feelings was a major contributor to his breakdown. Times of isolation from loved ones seem particularly troubling to him.

I can say from my perspective that this recent behavior is definitely NOT characteristic of the preceding part of Jeremy's life history. It is my belief that with counseling and psychiatric treatment it will be a momentary unrepeated episode that does not resemble any of the rest of his life history either. This, it seems to me, is a very likely outcome so long as he is helped to deal with his illness in a supportive environment. In my opinion, for what it's worth, Jeremy will respond well to a required regimen of regular therapy and as normal as possible routine otherwise in the loving atmosphere of his family here. Given all I know about his prior life experience, I feel really positive about his prospects going forward.

Sincerely,

Michael Qualls

Michael Qualls
Organizing Pastor

501-835-8889

1402 E. Kiehl Ave.
Sherwood, AR 72120

A true FRIEND is a real FIND!

(The letter of support written by our pastor. There were a few other letters from friends and family members. Two from my mother, both of which are too long to add here. Sorry, mom. The book was also filled with family photos, stories of my childhood, and all of my military achievements. The address in the bottom right corner is the location of the church that I walked into when I finally made it to central Arkansas from Arizona.)

Wisconsin

As I write this paragraph today, I have lived with the diagnosis of bipolar for twenty-one years. Mentally and emotionally it has been a very rocky twenty-one years. Many highs and lows. During those years I have given up on my medications numerous times, which led to more manic episodes, although nothing like the big kahuna of all episodes. I have stopped medications for various reasons. Sometimes I felt I didn't need them. Sometimes I didn't like the side effects I was experiencing. Other times I didn't think they were working. But mostly I stopped taking them because I didn't want to accept the fact that I would have to rely on them to function properly for the rest of my life. After witnessing numerous times what my mental state is like when not on the medications, I've realized that my life is better with them. And if you are suffering from mental distress I sincerely hope you are able to come to that realization as well.

When you first start having mental behavioral episodes or changes, it's almost impossible to recognize them yourself. But after you've been through a few you can sometimes notice what's about to happen before it gets in full manic or depressive mode. For me, when a manic episode is coming on, the first thing I notice is that I get agitated very easily, by anything. Even things that I usually enjoy will agitate and bother me somehow. Next is my sleep. It gets harder and harder to get any amount of sleep. This is due to my mind racing. A racing mind is a classic sign of bipolar mania, and sleep is often the first thing affected.

Next, I start to lose control of my emotions. And I can no longer gather myself or 'pull myself back together'. I lose this ability because again, my mind is racing so fast that I can't focus on anything else, including my emotions. We've all had those moments where you're having a great time with others only for it to be interrupted by something like a small argument with someone or a significant other. And before you can go back and be around everyone else, you have to gather your emotions back together and put on a great face as if that small argument never happened. Well, with bipolar, you can't gather yourself back up or put yourself back together to seem stable to others. No ability at all. I can't stress this enough.

Sometimes I know when a depressive episode is lingering because I start to get over-emotional, about everything. Everything will make me sad. Commercials on TV. Stray pets around town. Homeless people. During a depressive episode, seeing these things will make me numb and I'll tremble. Everything around me ceases to exist and it's like I can only concentrate on that one thing. I know I shouldn't be crying at the squirrel in the road that got hit by a car. But the disorder makes me see how sad it is, that life was taken and will no longer exist for that animal. Not only does bipolar force those emotions on me, but it amplifies them.

"You will cry, and you will cry now! Do it!"

And I bawl like a baby.

Why? Because the wiring and chemicals in my brain are abnormal. Your brain controls your body in every aspect. Once bipolar is at its peak, whether it be depression or mania, you are along for the ride. You cannot 'suck it up and get over it'. The person going through this episode does not have the ability to make that choice. Even if they could, mental illness of any kind is not something that you can just *get over*. If you are a person reading this who has never had bipolar, the one thing I ask that you take away from this story, and the disorder itself, is that the person going through the depressive or manic episode has absolutely no control over any aspect of either episode.

They don't need you to tell them to 'just suck it up and get over it'. They don't need to hear that they are exaggerating or overreacting because during these episodes they can't do either. Eventually, these episodes can be noticed early on and the person can initiate behavioral therapy, breathing exercises, or take as-needed medication. But those things don't stop the episode, they just make the episode manageable. Hopefully.

The. Person. Experiencing. The. Episode. Does. Not. Have. Control. Of. The. Episode.

Bipolar disorder can be a result of a chemical imbalance in the brain, stresses in life, genetics, traumatic experiences, and even medications, drugs, and alcohol. Now ask yourself, how is a person supposed to 'just get over' having a chemical imbalance in their brain? Or 'just get over' a traumatic event? And to those of you that do suffer from any kind of mental illness and have been told to 'just suck it up', or 'get over it already', please distance yourself from that person immediately. You will be doing yourself and your recovery an enormous favor.

When I was diagnosed, I was simply diagnosed. That was it. I was told what I had and given medication for it. I was given great help in person, but I wasn't given instructions on how to recognize my disorder for the long term or how to deal with any symptoms once I left these psychiatric facilities. Sadly, mental healthcare for active duty soldiers, at that time, was not great at all. Only in the last few years has a focus on mental health become prominent in the military and civilian world. 'Take these pills and go' was pretty much the gist of my outpatient care.

Now, back to that day in court. When you go to court and the judge tells you 'you're free to go', you're not really free to go anywhere at that moment, except back to where you came from. You have to sit and wait for every other case to be heard. You have to be chained back up to rapists and gang members. You have to get back in a van and ride back to the county jail. Then you have to sit and wait, sometimes days, until everything is in place for you to go to your next destination. I remained in the county jail for almost a week until I was picked up to go to the state hospital. In total, I was in the Pulaski County jail for approximately ninety-five days. I now had another sixty days to go in the state hospital.

My opinion of the state hospital upon first arrival was not great. It looked like where psychiatric patients go to be tested on until their dying days because society has rejected them.

That opinion would soon be changed.

Nebraska

The process of entering and going through the motions of becoming a new patient at a psychiatric institution can be hard, for anyone. *New* is hard for a lot of people, no matter what it is referring to. Not only are you in this new and lonely place with a bunch of strangers, but you're completely lost as to what exactly is wrong with you. Am I severely mentally unstable? I mean, I've been sent to the Arkansas State Hospital. Am I going to be living in an institution for the rest of my life? This thought of course entered my mind numerous times. Did I just go from a soldier defending his country to a felon to a mental patient in a matter of four months? Integrating into a psychiatric facility while also trying to learn what is wrong with you is extremely hard. You're around people you've never met. You have very strict rules to learn and follow. You have classes and activities you have to attend and participate in, no matter how uncomfortable they are. And when all of that is over, you go to your room, lay in your bed, and try to cope with what exactly is wrong with you mentally.

Most of the time, what's going through your head is too hard to explain to the doctors and therapists, the majority of whom have never been through what you might be going through. You can't explain or express the feelings, the emotions, the sensations. They are new to you. The feelings you experienced, or are experiencing, are sometimes so terrible that it feels like there aren't words that have been created that can explain those feelings accurately. The emotions are so powerful that they overwhelm you to the point that you can't keep track of what happened or what is happening. You may have an idea of how depressed and sad you feel, or how hyper you feel during your manic episode. But when it comes time to sit face to face with a doctor and explain those feelings, you have absolutely no clue what to say. And at that moment, when you can't find the words to describe your emotions, you feel even more helpless and lost. Not only are you now in a mental institution trying to figure out what happened or what is happening, but you can't even tell this doctor what you're feeling because the emotions are so extravagant. So you sit there as a feeling of complete worthlessness takes over your entire body.

Please be advised that I am not a doctor or therapist of any kind. I'm simply a patient. These ideations are of course just my opinion and an overview of what I experienced and felt.

Life in the state hospital was hard, mentally and emotionally. I spent most days in denial because my bipolar episode had been over for almost four months now and I was under the impression that I was done with it. I was warned it would come back, maybe even worse than before. It was crucial that I stayed on medications.

"For how long?"

"The rest of your life."

"#$@%!"

I was also told that I may never have another bipolar episode ever again, manic or depressive. Well, that would be awesome. But this is me we're talking about. Of course I'm going to have another episode. There's that glass half empty thinking again. Damn it, Jeremy!

The state hospital turned out to be the best thing for me and provided more help than I had received from anywhere else. Sixty days was a long time. But it was definitely better than the alternative. I wasn't going to prison, and I have been thankful for that to this day. If I had gone to prison I would have been released about ten years ago. The most alarming thing about that for me is that if I had gone then my sons aren't born. It is mind-boggling to think how decisions we make and instances throughout our lives affect what happens to our future, and the future of others.

If the judge hadn't approved the plan that was presented in court, my sons are not here. They do not exist. I am not a father. My mother has two fewer grandchildren. If the judge had said 'denied', I would have been in prison in 2005 and 2007, which is when they were born. Thankfully that didn't happen, but it is crazy and alarming to think about. I'm so grateful for how everything turned out and for everyone who helped me during that time. There is no way I could have done any of that by myself.

When you think of the phrase 'state hospital', you probably think of people walking around and mumbling while others are drooling all over themselves due to tons of medications. At least those were my thoughts on the van ride over from the county jail.

It wasn't like that at all, *if* you followed the rules. Now I will say that they did have padded rooms, but no straight jackets. Instead of straight jackets they strapped you to a gurney and put you in the padded room until you shut up. If you started screaming again when they opened the door they simply shut the door and waited longer. I don't know this from personal experience. I know this because the room they put people in was across the hall from my sleeping quarters. On my tip toes, I could see through the window on my door and into the window of the padded room door. Occasionally I could see a shoulder or arm jerking about, but that was it.

At this point, it had already been over three months since my manic episode. I was calm. I was collected. I was still completely lost as far as what happened and how I was going to cope with this disorder for the rest of my life. But the worst was hopefully behind me, and I was on the upswing. I was very active in classes and activities. The first week you are not allowed to do much extracurricular stuff because they need to monitor you and make sure you don't try and climb the twenty-foot fence that surrounded us, which one woman actually tried to do.

After the first week, I was allowed to go to the gym and play…. you guessed it, basketball. I am so at ease on the basketball court. There are no worries in life. When I was playing basketball I didn't have bipolar. I hadn't just spent three months in jail. None of that existed in my head. I looked forward to those ninety minutes in the recreation center every day. It was a great escape and a wonderful coping mechanism. I highly recommend anyone with any kind of mental illness to pick up a hobby. It may take a while for you to find one that fits you, but when you find it you'll know. I truly hope you can find something that helps you escape what you have been burdened with.

Distraction can sometimes be great for your recovery. Just make sure you don't distract yourself so much that the distraction completely covers up your disorder.

You want your disorder to always be visible to you.

Hawaii

Overall, being in the state hospital wasn't too bad. There were patients of all ages and walks of life. All of us had behavioral disorders and majority were criminals of some kind. We all wore the same green hospital scrubs. During the day we were kept busy with classes, discussions, therapy sessions, and activity time in the gym. You had a break in the afternoon and a few cigarette breaks throughout the day. Including me, there were around twenty people in my section of the hospital. It was a pretty relaxed environment. The nurses and staff interacted with us during downtime and tried their best to treat us like humans instead of patients.

It was a coed unit. And yes, *things* happened. Psychiatric patients still have needs after all. Let's just be honest here, sex is a great stress reliever and distraction. I didn't think twice about putting myself and my health in that position, but it happened among other patients. And the majority didn't really bother trying to hide it. Evenings on the unit weren't much fun. Once activity time at the gym was over and you'd showered and stuff there were still two to three hours to kill until lights out. There was a TV in the dayroom, which not many others watched except me. It was a great distraction. The amazing and circus-like play of the Sacramento Kings basketball team always kept my mind occupied.

Vlade Divac, Chris Webber, Mike Bibby, and others were so exciting to watch on the basketball court. It was almost like watching the Globetrotters. All the way to the dayroom I would pray that no one else was using the TV. My eyes would light up as soon as I noticed that the TV was off. Now this was 2003, and the TV was older than that. So there wasn't streaming TV or a Roku device. I had to find the channels using the dials on the TV. Yes, dials. You actually had to turn a knob to the channel you wanted. I would pull up what looked to be a loveseat right in front of the TV, then I'd kind of turn in the fetal position with my feet over one end and fade off into TV bliss. For a little while I wasn't a patient. I wasn't a criminal.

For me, the worst part of any psychiatric stay is nighttime. Once the charge nurse yelled for everyone to be in their rooms, all of that bliss went away. Now I was in my bed, alone. I was actually in a four-person room with no other patients. I would have preferred at least one other person in there with me to shoot the breeze with. When you're in jail or the state hospital you're constantly searching for things to occupy your time. Once in bed and the ward lights faded, a feature film of my life would project onto the ceiling above. Memories, good or bad. Lifetime achievements. Any and everything would flash through my mind for what felt like hours.

I saw many things on my ceiling. With each blink of my eyes, a different moment in time would appear. Fond memories of family gatherings. Church youth group events. Me singing in church. My first kiss. That time I was intentionally knocked to the floor during a church league basketball game and had to be rushed to the ER in an ambulance. Church league basketball is vicious. I saw myself picking blackberries on the farm. Military achievements. I saw myself, my brother, and my cousins taking turns starting at the top of Uncle Harold's barn and sliding down to see how close we could get to the edge without falling off.

I fell off.

Aunt Sis came running out because she had been watching our ridiculous behavior. I was okay. I survived a lot of things on the farm. My life movie would cut from that scene and immediately go to the embarrassing scene of me making a joke about Dolly Parton's breasts. I was in the backseat with one of my teenage girlfriends while her mother and stepdad sat up front. I don't know why Dolly was brought up, and I don't remember what I said. But I remember the car going uncomfortably quiet and my girlfriend looking embarrassed. I called her stepdad the next day and apologized, due to her urging of course. I'm sure I was too much of a boy to realize the totality of the situation. I distinctly remember laying in bed at the state hospital and that memory flashing before me. Maybe it was my mind mustering up some strength to force some funny moments into my head. Wonderful moments like family trips to Gulf Shores, sitting and watching my mother on stage singing at a festival at Burns Park, and countless fishing trips with Dad were also broadcast on the ceiling above. The mind has a way of trying to make you feel better sometimes.

Did some of those memories or occurrences in my past cause me to be where I am now? Traumatic events can ignite bipolar. Well, two instances of suicide in the family would sure count as traumatic events. Were their decisions to end their own lives the beginning of what put me here today? Not that I would ever blame my brother and father in any way for anything. But laying in bed late at night with a racing mind, you ponder about things like that. At least I did. Could their bouts with mental anguish have ignited my bout with mental anguish? Like I said in chapter two, my mind is a complete mess.

I also remember seeing the image of me sitting between a toilet and a bathroom stall divider while crying my eyes out after just being told my father had died. I was probably in there for a good thirty minutes or so. Someone, I don't know who, opened the bathroom door and asked if I was okay. I mustered up the best 'yes' that I could and they quickly closed the door and let me be. I cried until my chest hurt. When you've been given that kind of news it's almost as if your mind starts to glitch. It's trying to process the terrible news you just received while also trying to construct the emotions you should feel from that news, and it's trying to do both at the same time. It's like a 'check brain' light comes on.

But why? What happened? Why now? When? Where? How? Are you sure? Is my father really gone? I just saw him two weeks ago and he seemed fine. Why didn't he say something to me?

I had so many questions running through my head so fast,

while at the same time experiencing numerous emotions all at once. You feel so lost during that moment. It's overwhelming. My body's first reaction was to throw up. I barely made it from the office to the bathroom next door without vomiting. Once my stomach was emptied, I collapsed between the toilet and the divider and leaned my head over the seat so the blood from my nose wouldn't get all over the floor. I was crying so uncontrollably that I was choking on my saliva. Every part of my body from my chest up was instantly thrust into overdrive. It felt as if my lungs couldn't keep up with the amount of crying that came flowing out of me like an opened dam. My breathing would interrupt my crying. My crying would interrupt my breathing. I was sitting on the floor of one bathroom stall dry-heaving for each breath, while my legs were spread into another stall. It's like the wind had been knocked out of me. I had to raise my arms above my head to gain any kind of control of my breathing. My father taking his own life had sucked the life out of me.

There weren't going to be any more fishing trips.

My sister Teresa and I playing in the very pool I would clean for my grandparents during my teenage summers. Sixteen years after this photo she would call to inform me that our father had succumbed to mental hardships.

Ohio

Life. It can be a wonderful thing. For some. There are so many aspects of life that you can immerse yourself in. You can travel the world and experience different cultures. You can raise a family and share wonderful moments with them. You can further your education and teach and inspire others. You can be a nomad and live off the grid and envelop yourself with nature. There are endless possibilities with each waking hour of your existence. Those possibilities are available to you because you passed the ultimate test. You were the one sperm out of millions that won the race to the egg. Millions! Nine months later you were a full-fledged human being, in a womb, alive yet protected from the world. Then oxygen from the Earth entered your lungs for the first time as you cried out. Your body immediately started functioning on its own. You were born. You were granted life. Breath. Existence. The chance to experience Earth. To grow. To learn. To work. To relax. To laugh. And to love.

For some people, every day from their birth can be nothing but a battle. All the time. Traveling the world may not interest you. Raising a family or sometimes even being around family may seem overwhelming to you. You might not have any motivation to advance any aspect of your life. Living a life of loneliness, sorrow, and depression is all that you see in your future. You see and believe these things because it seems that's all you've ever been through. You get used to it. The negativity grows into normalcy. Disorders have a way of slowly taking over one's life. So slow that you don't even know that it's happening. You become manipulated and enslaved by it. It's gained so much control that you believe without a doubt that you cannot rise back up from the depths it's forced you into. Living in those depths is hard, but it's easier than battling the disorder every day. So you give up. You give in.

I can honestly say that during the last twenty-one years of living with bipolar that most of those days have been extremely hard. Not an overwhelming percentage, but the majority have been very difficult. I have given up and given in many times throughout those twenty-one years. And I will most likely do so again at some point down the road. During those years, my disorder has taken many things from me. My purpose. My faith, in anything. The ability to make my own decisions, and the ability to understand the consequences of bad decisions. Bipolar forced its fist into my chest and ripped every emotion out of me. I have been to the deepest and darkest depths of bipolar depression. I have seen black so dark that the person mixing paint at Home Depot wouldn't be able to match it.

Fortunately, these days I have a grasp on all of those things. Not a firm grasp, but a grasp. The one thing my disorder took from me that dealt the biggest blow was my emotions. Without emotions, of any kind, you feel so hollow. So useless. I felt like that one white crayon in the box that never gets used because no one ever wants it. No one needs it. It serves no purpose. My mind was a white crayon and my life was a white sheet of paper. It's a very desolate state to be in. Thankfully, I can now recognize and experience all emotions. But because I've been living with bipolar for so long, I now question my emotions often. I wish I didn't do this. I wish my reactions to my emotions were more natural. I wish I could just let them be a part of me and let them take over my body how they're supposed to, whether they be happy or sad emotions.

That movie kind of made me sad. Wait, is that bipolar telling me to be sad or am I naturally feeling sad? Is that sadness going to lead to a depressive state?

It's a terrible way to live. I don't do this intentionally. It's a habit that has developed over time because I'm scared of falling into another manic or depressive state. Sadly, I spend most of my days on mental guard. It's not *if* I will experience bipolar symptoms today, it's how many symptoms and how severe will they be. The most honest and true emotion I remember feeling prior to my children being born was when my father died. Those emotions took complete control over every ounce of my body. From his death to the beginning of my manic episode was roughly five years. The first couple of years after my father's death seemed okay to me. I thought I handled them well. But I didn't. Quite the opposite in fact.

I ended up pushing his death aside, refusing to accept it. Being transferred to serve a year in South Korea I think was the tipping point that sent my mental state overboard. To myself, I seemed okay. My work performance was great. I was physically fit. I didn't feel depressed. Life seemed great. But not dealing with my father's death and then also not confronting the stress of being in Korea eventually took its toll. I wasn't stationed in a hazardous area or anything like that. But being shipped off to South Korea at twenty-one right after losing my father definitely had an effect on me. And the longer I put his death aside the worse the eruption of bipolar was going to be. Looking back now from my current point of view, I can slowly see instances throughout time where my life started to slowly crumble away.

As soon as I arrived home from Korea in December of 2000, I got married. No, I'm not saying marriage contributed to making things crumble away. But months later at Fort Huachuca, we were already seeing a military marriage counselor. She and I weren't physical with each other. Some of the problems were her being away from home for the first time in her life and not understanding that I wouldn't be home a lot due to military training exercises and such. Some of it was my inability to realize that I was now in a serious relationship, my first ever, and that certain decisions required input from both of us. I have realized that I made those decisions without her input due to bipolar. I didn't have the ability to understand the consequences of making those decisions on my own because my mind would race so much that I couldn't stop it long enough to acknowledge the consequences. Making that decision on my own, and knowing the outcome, provided the rush that my disorder needed to survive. It wasn't that I wanted control of the relationship, I've never been that type of person, it was that bipolar wanted control. And it was slowly getting that control with every rash decision I would make.

The counseling was more for guidance than anything. We were young and had no clue what we were doing. We both needed help with the new situation we were in. Looking back I'm glad we got that help. At the time, I had no idea what was slowly brewing in my head. Decades later I can now see that bipolar was causing most of our relationship problems. Most of my rash decision-making problems revolved around spending money. Impulsive spending is one of the top symptoms of bipolar mania. Write that down. This symptom was the most prolific symptom at the beginning of my bipolar episode. An episode that took several years to finally boil over.

If I wanted to get new furniture, it had to be done. If I wanted to buy a scooter so both of us had transportation, it had to be done. If I wanted a pair of shoes that I would never wear, I had to buy them. Not because I wanted the new car or because I needed a scooter to get around the base, but because of the rush I got from the impulsive spending decision.

It's important to know all of the symptoms. Learn them, (I've put some in the back of this book). Keep an eye out for them. It's also important to monitor yourself every day, even on good days. Get a diary and write down things that happened that were good and also things that were bad. Make a logbook in your phone. Do something that helps you keep up with things you do and things that happen to you every day. Anything that allows you to look back and see where things may have gone off the rails. Maybe something happened right before a manic episode started. A trigger. A traumatic event. It's great to have daily routines and instances written down so you can go back and look and see exactly what was going on in your life at the time an episode may have started.

My time at the state hospital was nearing its end. I was about to be introduced back into the world. I was about to be a civilian. Something I hadn't been for over five years.

Something I thought I'd never be again.

Connecticut

There are periods in life where you stop worrying about why you're here and just live in the moment and whatever happens happens. For the first time in my life, this was how I felt after leaving the state hospital. This was surprising to me because I've always been addicted to figuring out my purpose. I have to know my reason for waking up the next day. It's something that I am constantly trying to grasp. It's just my nature. I don't want my existence to just be the result of a sperm race. I need to know that what I am doing is meaningful. That what I'm doing is worth something. That *I'm* worth something.

Part of the reason I wasn't worried about my purpose at that point was because I had given up on myself. How could I possibly bounce back from all of this and live a normal life, let alone figure out my purpose? My life's reason was the last thing on my mind. When I left the state hospital I had no idea who I was. I was completely lost, in every aspect of life. Mentally, physically, emotionally. I had just been through a terrible bipolar episode, months of jail time, and a state hospital stay, only to be thrust into the world with what I felt was nothing.

Hey! You're bipolar. Good luck!

I had never felt so useless and lost. But luckily I was addicted to something, my purpose. It wasn't on my mind at that point, but over time it would slowly become a part of everyday life again. I honestly believe my drive to find and know my purpose is part of the reason I am where I am today. It provided motivation. It now felt like finding my purpose was my purpose. If it was going to be a lifelong search then I was okay with that. It had been a crazy ride over the last few months. It was now time to go on a safer Sunday drive through the rest of my life. Hopefully.

Now I don't remember actually leaving the hospital or even who came and picked me up. But I remember thinking many times during the months after everything was over how lucky I was to be where I was, even if it included serious mental disorders. I was living in my mother's home that she was trying to sell. She was now living elsewhere. I think she had moved while I was in jail. So luckily I had a place to go once I was released from the state hospital. In the coming months, my bipolar would show its face here and there. I got this bright idea to paint one of her bedrooms this awful bright shade of blue. Yes, blue. This is one of the things that bipolar does to me. It puts these ridiculous thoughts into my head and I do them. Do you know those decorative ends of curtain rods? Well, I got this bright idea to buy two huge round ones and screw them into the corners of her master bathroom countertops.

She was pissed.

But this is what happens when my symptoms come to the forefront. Not only does it make decisions for me, it prevents me from seeing the result of those decisions. I'm not allowed to see the result. If I saw the result then the mania wouldn't get fed. I battled a few bipolar flareups once I was back home but nothing major. Using my military experience I eventually landed a security job. Yes, someone actually hired me. I had to drive forty-five minutes to Pine Bluff at five in the morning. The pay wasn't great, but with everything I had just gone through, I wasn't going to complain. I was grateful for where I was and what I had at the time. It was either this or prison. I had a job, a nice place to stay, and a family for support. I was happy.

However, soon after leaving the state hospital, I stopped taking my medications. There was no way I was going to live the rest of my life according to pills. Absolutely not. I wanted a life free of medications. A life where I made my own choices. A life that was mine, that didn't belong to disorders or pills. I wanted free will. I wanted to have a purpose again. I wanted reason. And I felt bowing down to daily pills and therapy wasn't going to allow me to have any of that. I had to take the pills to have some kind of control over my brain. At the time I refused to acknowledge this. I was Superman again.

I am *not* taking those pills! *No one* can tell me what to do!

Except for Mom, she made me repaint that blue bedroom.

At that time, my mind was 100% dependent upon the medications. I did not see it that way. I couldn't see it that way. I could not see that I needed pills to make proper daily decisions. Not taking pills and putting my bipolar on the back burner was probably a decision made by my bipolar disorder. In my mind, doing away with the pills was the right thing to do. It showed I could make decisions for myself, no matter how stupid they were. But I was only fooling myself. Months would go by with no medication. Now and then I would recognize some mania symptoms but I was able to control them, somewhat. In the coming months, I would be off and on Depakote. Sometimes I would give in and take them for a few weeks then I would grow tired of them and all they would do was piss me off. A few times when I saw that bottle of pills on my nightstand I would grab it and throw it across the room. Being told you can't live a normal life without medication is demoralizing. It kills your pride. It stifles your yearning for a regular life.

In the coming months, my grandfather would pass away. The same grandfather I had deceived and tricked and stolen from. Not on medication, I had the audacity to show up at his funeral as if I had done nothing to him just seven months prior. I sat in the back of the funeral home and stood far away from others outside at the burial ceremony. I knew there were a few people there that didn't want me there. But it was my grandfather. I wasn't going to let them stop me from paying my last respects to a man who taught me so much and kept me out of trouble by offering me so much work when I was young. I stole from him. I put him in a helpless and confusing position at an old age. But two years prior, when he was eighty, this man drove in the dark to my wedding. I was going to give this man the respect I felt he deserved, no matter how many dirty looks I knew I was going to get during the ceremony.

I was now a part-time security guard with bipolar disorder and I had no clue what I was doing with my life. No clue what the future held. I was starting from scratch. Just months ago I had everything. A job I loved. A purpose that I woke up excited for every day. Now I was back to square one. I was twenty-five and had no clue what direction I needed to be going or even what direction I wanted to go. I know what you're thinking, not many people know what they want to be doing with their life by age twenty-five. Well, I did. And it was taken from me by things beyond my control. Not only did I now have to restart my life and find some kind of purpose, but I had to do it while also dealing with bipolar.

I had everything. Comfort. Security. Self worth. Self-esteem. Good health. A promising career that I was quickly advancing in. I knew what my future was going to be. I had no worries about any of that. I was going to be in the Army until I turned thirty-eight. Then I was going to retire and get a part-time job somewhere and take a few vacations a year until I passed on. My life was on cruise control. Until it wasn't. I crashed and burned.

I felt like I had just been dragged through life, thrown in a truck, and dumped next to the burn pile where the high school kids hang out after football games. But I had been given what many others are not, another chance. As much trouble as my bipolar had gotten me into, and as far out of reach as my purpose in life seemed, there I was, starting over, from the bottom. I didn't flinch. I didn't give up. As soon as I got out of the hospital I started looking for a job. I had to keep pushing. The opposite scared me. I had just been through something that I never wanted to go through again. My purpose had been a motivating factor all throughout my life. I had found it. It was then taken from me. I could never re-enlist in the Army again to resume that purpose. I had to find another. I had to know my reason. It's instilled in me. Being given the rare opportunity to be on this earth and then doing nothing noteworthy while you're here isn't going to look great at the pearly gates, at least that's how I see it.

"So...Mr. Hughes. What have you done with your life that is worthy of acceptance into heaven?"

"Well...umm...you see...what happened was..."

"Mr. Hughes.......?"

"Funny thing,....."

"Purgatory!"

Iowa

I've asked my sons many times what they want to be when they grow up. Neither has ever given me an actual answer. They like video games and playing basketball. I've suggested being a video game designer. They always just mumble along, seemingly just to get me to shut up about it. Why am I so addicted to my purpose? Why do I need that assurance? Why do I need proof of my existence? Why can't I be comfortable with just being whatever I end up being? Why can't I just mumble along and forget about it like my kids do? I honestly think that being diagnosed with bipolar has made my obsession with my purpose even more apparent. It's as if I'm wearing a sign stating I have bipolar and I have to walk around with it every day, spending every second of my life proving that I'm something more than a mental patient.

Yes, I may be bipolar, but look what I may become! Don't look at my disorder. Look at me!

Like the Matchbox Twenty song says….

"I'm not crazy, I'm just a little unwell, I know, right now you can't tell. But stay a while and maybe then you'll see, a different side of me."

Everyone who has ever known me now knows me as that person who had a mental breakdown. I'm that guy who went crazy and stole a bunch of stuff and broke into someone's home. Sadly, at my funeral, this is what some people will remember. And sadly, I can't change that. I guess that's why I'm even more obsessed now with my reason. I guess I feel like I have to change the narrative.

I'm not a bipolar patient! I'm this! I'm that!

I've never been one to care what others think of me. I'm not going to let someone's opinion of me ruin even just a second of the time I've been granted on this Earth. Means nothing to me. However, maybe I'm subconsciously obsessed with my purpose so I seem accomplished in the eyes of others. That could very well be. And I've never thought of that until writing this paragraph. Thanks, me. My biggest fear is failure. Failing myself. Failing my family, something I've already done many times. Or failing my children. It pains me to think about me being eighty-five, sitting on the couch having no clue what I'm watching on the TV, and looking back on my life and realizing I never found my purpose. What a waste that would be.

In the months and years after being released from the state hospital, I would have numerous jobs. Each eventually leading to another better job. During this time I would meet the mother of my sons. Our oldest was born in September of 2005, and our youngest in June of 2007. We had our first child just over two years after I left the state hospital. I had been on and off medication during those two years. I was far from mentally stable. I was stable enough to hold a job and help with parenting, but occasionally I would make rash decisions and stupid choices here and there. We moved a few times and I switched jobs numerous times. I would go from delivering pizzas to being an assembly technician. Eventually, I ended up getting a great job with a medical delivery company. We delivered specialty beds and other items to local hospitals. I'm extremely grateful for that company giving me a chance after what I had gone through from a judicial standpoint.

Life was going pretty smoothly. All seemed okay. We settled into a nice, small home in the southwest part of Jacksonville, AR. We had our ups and downs as most do, but nothing dramatic or anything we couldn't push through. However, a few things hit us all at once and we just couldn't work through them all. In 2009 she and I eventually split up. And according to Arkansas law, the mother automatically gets the children, even though I was the one with the job and a way to support them. I was devastated. I immediately fell into a deep depression due to losing the children and the lack of time I got to see them. This was the deepest depression I had ever been in, and the second depressive state that I ever remember having. I didn't sleep for the first few days that my children were gone, and I was unable to work due to the lack of sleep. When I came back to work I told my boss about what was going on with my kids and somehow I let it slip that I had stopped taking some medications. He basically forced me into a two-week notice. The best job that I had since the military was now gone.

Since the moment I lost my father, losing my children was the most devastating thing that had ever happened to me. It hit me harder than anything I had ever experienced. Taken. Gone. Just like that. One day I'm walking in the door to them running up to me as they scream in excitement. The next day the house is completely silent. It was instant darkness. I was in bed all day, every day. I could no longer see them when I wanted. I no longer heard their babbling and laughing throughout the house. All I could hear was silence. The sound of pain. Their mother automatically had full custody and could choose when and where I saw them. I had no choice in anything. She let them visit with me here and there but I'd say 85% of the time they were with her.

My depressive state got so bad that I eventually started abusing marijuana. I'm talking about *heavy* marijuana use. All day. At this point in my life, I was thirty years old and smoking pot 24/7. It was an escape. With each exhale, clouds of smoke would provide a protective fog from the reality that my children were no longer in my life. Before this, the only bad thing involving drugs or alcohol in my life was when I stole a few beers from Dad so I could take them on a church youth group trip. Like I told you earlier in the story, I was the bad kid.

I had already lost my job and my children. I would eventually lose my apartment and be homeless. I would bounce around from one friend's home to the next. Sometimes I lived in my car in hotel parking lots in between stays at friend's houses. I would fold down the back seats and sleep with half of my body in the trunk and half in the back seats. I was off medication and smoking weed all day, daily. So much to the point I was losing weight at an alarming rate. My face was sunk in and my limbs looked like twigs. The smoking would become worse and worse. The more I couldn't see my sons the worse each day became. I was smoking myself out of existence. I would have a joint before I had breakfast. I was so upset with where I was in life. My brother and father taken, my military purpose taken, jail time, state hospital, being forced to start all over from the bottom. Despite all of that, I dug deep to create a foundation for the next chapter of my life. But my children would be taken from me before I could finish the framework. If I didn't have them, I didn't have anything.

Have I not worked hard enough for all of the trials to be over? What do I have to do to figure out and live out my purpose?! How much more am I going to be tested? Have I not proven myself? Or is all of this deserved for some reason?

Things got so bad that I gave in to peer pressure and the marijuana eventually led to meth.

Once.

It scared me so much that I never did it again.

Being on meth is basically like having a 150 heart rate, being chased by cops, walking in the door and watching TV for two seconds, and then getting the bright idea to refold and stack everything in the linen closet while a giant gorilla paces behind you, all at the same time. It was the closest to death that I had ever felt in my life. Every second you feel like your heart is about to stop even though it's beating uncontrollably. You get that feeling of impending doom that some say you get right before a heart attack. Well, when you're on meth, you have that feeling every second until the drug wears off.

Please do not give in. I beg you. From first-hand experience, I can honestly say that meth is not the escape you want. Marijuana is not the escape you want. Yes, reality can be a bitch sometimes, but you don't need that kind of cover. You don't need drug-colored glasses to shield you from the negative aspects of life. I promise you.

We all need an escape now and then. Just choose it wisely.

Maine

Having kids and being their father was such a joy. I always looked forward to the end of the work day so I could rush home knowing they would be running to the door to greet me. They put a smile on my face every day. I believe they saved me in a way. I see them as an offering to try and finish what my father wasn't able to. My dad was not the gold standard of fathers, but he wasn't the opposite either. He was a busy man. A confused man. A mentally lost man. But he did the best he could. I'm sure all of his struggles affected his parenting abilities. I'm sure he wanted to be more involved in our lives, his mental struggles just wouldn't allow it. The truth is, it was hard for him to be involved in anyone's life, even the general public.

I distinctly remember us going to Taco Bell one day after church. Dad was driving and Mom wanted him to go through the drive-thru. Well, Dad didn't want to do that. A small argument ensued and Dad eventually gave in and proceeded to drive up to the speaker to order. He was beyond upset and extremely uncomfortable. Why? At the time I had no idea. But looking back I can see how interacting with other people made him so uncomfortable. Just imagine being so overcome with mental hardships that you're reluctant to talk to someone through a drive-thru speaker. That small interaction with another human scares you. That's how bad things got for him. But he wasn't like that every minute of the day. If you said hello to him at church he'd greet you and gladly engage in conversation. It was just certain scenarios that made him feel very vulnerable and would cause him extreme panic. I can't imagine what it must have been like for my father to have wanted to be more involved in our lives but couldn't because his mind wouldn't allow it. Oftentimes, he couldn't even be involved in his own life.

My mental struggles are the opposite of what he went through. He battled major depression. I've battled extreme mania. I'm thankful it hasn't gotten in the way of daily interactions with my children or others. I do get slight anxiety attacks sometimes when I'm going to a place that I know is going to be busy, but I can eventually face it. My mania doesn't run my life on a daily basis. It doesn't steal time from my life like it used to. My boys have been through a lot, and they need everything I can provide. I'm thankful that my mania isn't so much of a factor these days and I can focus on their lives.

My sons being taken from me sent me into a downward spiral for a couple of years. My mother would eventually apply for and be granted custody of my sons. I was still not well mentally or physically, so I was in no shape to provide or care for them myself. So they moved to Tennessee and lived with her and my stepfather. They raised them for a few years for which I am truly grateful. Unfortunately, my marijuana use would continue. My refusal to take medications for my bipolar would continue. I would get well for a few months then I would falter again into a downward spiral. I would be on and off medication. On and off marijuana. Medication. Marijuana. I'd be at a friend's house for a few weeks. Hotel parking lots for a few weeks. Friends houses. Parking lots.

While my sons were at my mother and stepfather's home being raised without a biological parent for the first time, I was living through the worst phase of my life. I missed them so much. There are no words that can describe what it feels like to no longer have your children in your life. I can't type out that feeling, so I'm going to stop staring at the screen hoping a word will pop into my head that describes it. All I can say is that I hope it doesn't happen to you. Cherish every second you have with them. All of their happiness. Their sadness. Their curiosity. Their innocence. Soak all of that in. Before you can blink they will be taller than you and moving out of the house.

Eventually, things got to the point where I could no longer take not being around my children. My mother and stepfather graciously let me move in with them, a gesture that probably saved my life. I had put off asking to move in with them because my boys and my stepfather's mother were also living there. I figured I would have just been in the way. They didn't need that. They already had so much going on in their home. But I'm glad I decided to do it and even more glad they let me. I was so happy to be back around my boys every day.

I was now in my early thirties and living with family. No job. No money, except for the small disability pay I was getting from the Army. No belongings really. I had to give up most of my possessions when I lost the house because I had nowhere to put it all. I could have easily given up on life. Given up on my kids. Given in to my disorders. I'll be completely honest with you, I've thought about suicide. A few times. Not so much to the point where I thought about how I would do it or when and where. There's never been any specific ideas and I've never spent much time on the subject. But thoughts have entered my mind. I've been to those deep depths and have had to start over a few times in life. So yeah, thoughts have come and gone. But I'm here. I'm so scared of death that suicide doesn't concern me. I want to be here on this Earth every last second that I possibly can, even if I'm suffering a manic episode on my deathbed. I want every last second.

Bring them on!

While living with my mother and stepfather I slowly began to get better. I was able to get another security job where I worked the third shift. *Ugh...* I'd get home from work, take the kids to school, and then try my best to sleep during the day until it was time to pick them up in the afternoon. Seeing them as they came running out of the school doors towards me always made the day better. Everything wrong in my life was instantly right as soon as I saw their faces. They don't know what you've been through in life. They don't know if you're struggling or not. They don't know how tired you are from working third shift. All they know is that you're there. They're so innocent and free of everything, and that always made my life free of everything. As soon as we would get into the car they were already asking to be pulled in the wagon when we got home. I'd make them some snacks and we'd play outside until I was exhausted. Wagon rides were the norm. I probably pulled them around that neighborhood hundreds of times. It was great exercise, physically and mentally.

As time went on my bipolar would show up here and there. It was never too bad to the point where it ran my life or ruined my day all the time. But it occasionally popped its head out just to remind me that it was still there. Unfortunately, I would suffer my second major manic episode, which to this day is the last big episode I've had. My stepfather had been renovating their attic to turn it into an upstairs bedroom. It was taking weeks. Weeks turned into months. The drilling. The hammering. The sanding. The sawing. I could no longer take it and I made a rash decision. I had had enough. I packed up my stuff and left. In an instant, I was back to living in my car with no clue how I was going to survive, and worst of all, no kids. All of this because of some construction noise. This is what bipolar does to me. Sometimes I'm just not able to consider the consequences, no matter how bad they may be.

I had just abandoned my children. I moved to Tennessee because I could no longer go another day without them, and here I was leaving them. Something I probably never would have done if......I was on medication. I made my way back to central Arkansas. I cried all the way there while picturing their faces once they came to the realization that I wasn't coming home anymore. I wasn't going to be taking them to school or picking them up.

There weren't going to be any more wagon rides.

I immediately turned back to marijuana. Back to friend's houses and hotel parking lots. This would last for a few months until I eventually ended up living with my ex-wife. She graciously took me in and offered me shelter while I waited for my public housing application to be accepted. I picked up another pizza delivery job and helped her with bills and such. I was there for around seven months. I'm still so thankful to this day. Another gesture that probably saved my life.

On the day I received the call from public housing to let me know my home was available, I went and got the keys and moved in immediately. I bought an air mattress, a TV tray, and a radio. That's all that I had for about two months. But I had shelter. I had a place to call my own. It was at this point in my life that I realized I had been given many chances. Eventually one of these chances would be my last. I needed to take advantage of this opportunity before bipolar took advantage of me, again. I called the veteran's hospital and asked if I could do an immediate walk-in visit with a psychiatrist. I needed an ear. I needed to confess how I had been mistreating my disorder. I needed immediate help. And more importantly, I wanted help.

I was back on Depakote that same day. This was 2015. I would eventually get another job assembling items for retail stores. FYI: all of the grills and wheelbarrows and such that you see out in front of Home Depot are assembled by another company, not Home Depot employees. I would drive to Home Depot, Academy Sports, and other places and assemble these things. It was a great job that I loved. It wasn't great money but it was something. At that point in my life, I was lucky to have any job. Over the course of about a year, I was able to fully furnish the public housing condo. I had also been on medication for a good amount of time. My head seemed to be on straight. I was goal-oriented and doing everything I could in hopes of one day having my kids back living with me. After a long period of mental calmness, and after gaining traction financially, my mother let the boys move in with me.

Life was now back in alignment. Hopefully, it would last.

Bartlett Tennessee in front of my mother and stepfather's home. One of our daily wagon rides. You can see how skinny I was after smoking marijuana daily for so long.

Wyoming

Due to the chances of me having another bipolar episode, and the fact that I had a back injury from my military service that could leave me bedridden at any moment, my mother kept full custody of the boys but let them live with me. This way if it ever came to the point where I couldn't care for them they could just go back and stay with her. Legally it just made everything easier.

I had never been in the position of raising them completely on my own. There had always been another person there to help, whether it was their mother or my mother and stepfather. I was now on my own as a parent. A single parent battling two young boys while also battling bipolar? Parenting itself is hard enough. Parenting with bipolar is hell. But I was as ready as I would ever be for the fatherly mission. My purpose in life would have to wait. Or would it? I had two young boys to raise and care for, there wasn't time to be selfish and worry about all of that. I was content. Having them in my life was all I ever wanted. I was so excited to be back around them again. Before they came to live with me I had furnished their rooms with blankets and curtains featuring characters they liked. I bought all kinds of toys and books and gadgets for them. The county housing unit was small, and we didn't mind.

Love grows best in little houses.

Fortunately for me, parenting came somewhat naturally. I have a very hands-on approach when explaining and teaching them things. I think that aspect of my parenting comes from my time in the military. I already had experience guiding and setting an example for others. I think that experience really paid off and helped me dramatically in raising them. Instead of just telling them what I think they need to know, I like to use as many tools and visual aids as possible. I jump at the chance to teach them anything I may know, like rolling up an extension cord by wrapping it around your palm and underneath your elbow, something that my father taught me.

I've sat down with them many times and talked to them about drugs. I like to listen to the police scanner occasionally. Every time I hear a call for an overdose my heart aches and I immediately yell out for them and make them come listen. I want them to know how that kind of stuff can ruin and end lives. I want them to hear it firsthand. I've told them many times about adults who prey on young children. I've taken them out in the backyard and taught them how to use a fire extinguisher. How to change the oil in the car. How to change a tire. How to behave at the table. Every episode of 'Cops' that we watch together turns into a lecture. I take pride in teaching them every chance I can get.

The three of us being alone together was new to all of us. We were all learning many things, including how to deal with and live with each other. The last time I was living with the boys and raising them they were two and four years old, at this point of the story they are now ten and twelve. Things were completely different now. They had their own attitudes. Their own ways of doing things. They were becoming their own person with their own individuality and qualities.

As a parent, sometimes it's hard to accept that they no longer like the things you thought they liked. They don't want horses and turtles on their pillowcases, they want Transformers and sports teams. Seeing them grow and come into their own is a wonderful thing to witness. Letting go and realizing they aren't as dependent upon you as they used to be is very hard to accept. I didn't feel as needed as I did before. But at the same time, I was proud to see them doing things on their own. Well, doing the things they *wanted* to do on their own. You're still going to have to tell them four times to clean their bathroom before they actually do it. Just get used to it. I prepared as best I could for them to come stay with me, but I'll be honest, I was overwhelmed when they moved in. I now had a schedule to keep. Plans to follow. School stuff to keep up with. Making sure they were performing good hygiene. Taking them to dental and doctor's appointments. Cooking meals. Making their lunches for school. Taking them to the park. Helping them deal with life, friends, and peer pressure. Making sure they behaved well. Teaching them proper manners and how to treat and respect others. I honestly believe that the enjoyment I experienced with them every day was the inspiration to continue taking medication every night.

As of this very moment, my oldest is eighteen, is driving

himself to work, and is almost an inch taller than me. He naturally disagrees with most of what I say, as most eighteen-year-olds are supposed to do, yet has grown into a respectful young man that is kind and motivated. He's been working for four months now and has yet to miss a day of work or even show up late. He really enjoys having some responsibilities and he amazes me with his memory. He remembers my mother's wifi password from years ago. How is that possible? He definitely gets that from his mother. She was honor roll material in her school days. My youngest son is sixteen, he's in that lazy-to-responsible transition period. You know, where they love to help but only if they're asked. It's what sixteen-year-olds do. But he doesn't hesitate when I ask for his help with anything. He's very respectful as well. I can't remember the last time when I yelled across the house to get his attention and he didn't respond with 'sir?'. He is already equally as tall as me and has the funniest laugh ever. He has one of those laughs where the more he laughs, the more you laugh because of his laugh. And then he looks at you laughing and asks why you're still laughing. But you can't explain why you're laughing because you're laughing too hard at his laugh. He cracks me up. They have grown into great young men so fast. I know they'll both succeed at whatever life puts before them. We have been through so much together. Some extremely happy times. Some very rough times. Birthday parties. Sleepovers. Movie nights. A few pets along the way. Two fish died. Arguments. Fights between brothers. Voices raised. Rules broken. Lessons learned.

There have been moments where we've laughed together all night while playing Uno, which is our household pastime.

There have been times when we've screamed and yelled at each other during an argument until our voices were gone. We've experienced it all. They've taught me so much about life and myself. They have been a much-needed distraction from the mental chains that continue to try and hold me down to this day, and will every day for the rest of my life. My boys know I have bipolar. They know what it does to me. They don't know the inner workings or how much it can take control over a person, but they know Dad struggles sometimes. They know that mental disorders run in the family. They know that their grandfather and uncle took their own lives. They know I see a psychiatrist every few months. They see me take my pills every day.

And with each pill I take, I pray that they never have to take the same ones.

Or any for that matter.

New Mexico

As the years of living with bipolar have gone by, and even with my diagnosis having gotten much better, unfortunately, I have to say that not a day goes by that I don't think or worry about it. And that sucks! I have spent so many years in treatment and so many years on medications to try and get to a point where I have majority control of my illness, only to get to that point and worry about my illness of my own free will.

It's taken me so long to somewhat have a grasp on it and yet I voluntarily worry about it. What the hell is wrong with me?

It's as if the disorder messed me up so much when it was at full tilt that I'm constantly on guard. I can never be in the moment. It could be Thanksgiving dinner and I'm having a great time with the family. But during those few seconds of silence between conversations when I'm taking a moment to eat another bite, I'm thinking about how everyone is perceiving me at that very moment. Are they seeing me or are they seeing the bipolar me? Am I being me right now? Do I have full control of this very moment right now? This person I'm talking to knows what I've done. They most likely know I have mental disorders. Do they see something in the way I'm acting right now that I don't? Sometimes I'm afraid to be naturally sad about something because I've seen where sad can lead. I'm afraid to be naturally happy about something because I've seen where being happy and mania can lead. But I'm so grateful to be where I'm currently at mentally. I am light years beyond where I used to be. But now and then my disorder reminds me that it's still there. And it always will be.

And that sucks!

But that is my life.

And you know what? So what. I've accepted the hand I've been dealt. It took me many years to accept it but I finally did. I've accepted that I'm not perfect. I've accepted I never will be. I've accepted I've made mistakes and that I will make more. I've accepted I've failed and I will fail more. You also need to accept the fact that you're not perfect and that you never will be. You've made mistakes and you'll eventually make more. You've failed. And you will of course fail more.

Coming to these realizations will make them less painful when they actually happen. Having bipolar amplifies your reactions to your mistakes and your failures, at least for me anyway. Lack of control over my decisions was the symptom that bothered me the most. When my mind would race 150mph, I couldn't stop my thoughts long enough to concentrate on a single one of them. My thoughts would flip through the center of my head like that big wheel they spin on 'The Price Is Right'. Only my wheel never stops during a manic episode. Hundreds of thoughts. Thoughts about serious stuff. Thoughts about stupid stuff. What I did that day. What do I need to do tomorrow? Some stranger I saw at a donut shop ten years ago would flash into my memory and vanish.

What the hell was that about? Do I know that person?

The constant loss of control led me to the realization that I would rather live with medicated bipolar than live with un-medicated bipolar controlling every aspect of my life. I've been in the deepest depths of this disorder, as many others have. You may be there now while you're reading this and thinking to yourself, 'What the hell is this idiot talking about?' Heck, sometimes *I* don't even know what I'm talking about. This is chapter forty-four and I have no idea if I've made any sense to you up to this point. I'm just typing stuff out about what I've been through as it pops into my head. I'm no doctor. I'm no therapist. I'm no counselor. I'm also not a professional author. I have no degree or certificate in anything that has to do with mental health. I haven't been any of those things. But I've been something that's just as important as all of those. I've been a patient. I have experience. And in my opinion, nothing can substitute experience.

How many psychiatrists do you think have been at rock bottom as a patient in a psychiatric ward? My guess would be very few. That's not to say that they don't know what they're talking about and you shouldn't take them seriously. I mention the fact that I'm a mental patient in hopes that it carries weight with this book. Hopes that you'll take my story to heart because I've been as low as a human can mentally go.

I don't write all of this to brag as if I've rolled away a stone and risen from the depths of mental hardship. I write it as a testament that I've been where you might be right now, or where you've once been. I've been there. I know how dark it can get. I know how hard it can be just to breathe your next breath. I write this as an affirmation that recovering from mental tribulations can be done. Things can get better. Things will get better. But it's going to take time and lots of it. And it's going to take effort from you. And more than likely it will also take help from others. If you don't have others in your life then find some. The easiest way to find others is through your therapy sessions and meetings.

Bipolar affects different people in different ways. There is no mental blueprint. I hate to tell you this, but the original treatment you start with is most likely not going to be the treatment that helps you. It may help in some ways. But your treatment will probably be tweaked a few times along the way. Please come to that realization and be prepared for that. There's a good chance your medications will be changed. You may gain weight because of those medications. Depakote has added twenty pounds to my frame over twenty years. Are you honestly going to put aside your overall mental health and let the disorder have complete control of your life because you don't want to gain weight? If so, then I highly suggest mentioning that to your doctor. If your image and how others perceive you are more important than your overall mental well being then that is an issue that also needs attention.

If you are dealing with disorders of some kind I truly hope at some point you are able to see just how much they affect and control you. And I hope that you can see and know that you weren't put here to be depressed. You weren't put here to be sad every day. None of us were. But traumatic events happen in life that cause emotional and mental distress. Chemical imbalances can ignite and affect your mental state. It's nothing you did. It's nothing you failed at. It's not God signaling you out and punishing you. Please know this. Please realize this. It's really important for your treatment and overall well-being to know that you aren't at fault for these episodes and mental states.

You're most likely reading this because bipolar or another disorder has affected you or is currently affecting you in some way. Maybe directly or maybe because a family member or friend is bipolar. Maybe you're a doctor who wants to get a patient's viewpoint. Maybe you're just reading it because you're curious.

Whatever the reason, it's commendable.

New Jersey

One of the most important things you can do to help with your recovery is to be positive. I know, you're depressed. And you're probably asking yourself 'How am I supposed to be positive if I'm severely depressed?'

If I could be positive then all would be okay, genius.

I'm not saying to change your mood and thoughts positively, because in your current state, you most likely aren't capable of doing that. I'm simply saying to remind yourself to *try* and be positive. Positivity heals. I have seen it work a few times in my life. Negativity drains you, of all energy, physically and mentally. And remember, be patient with your positive thoughts. Be patient with every aspect of your recovery and treatment.

Put a Post-it note on your mirror with something positive on it.

Your hair looks great.

Set an alarm on your phone that has something positive in the notes section.

Hey, it's 3:30 p.m. You will get better.

Hey, it's 6:00 p.m. Smile.

Patience and understanding will be the keys to your mental treatment, in my opinion of course. I say that simply because those are the two main things that helped me. If you can learn to be patient and understand what your disorder does and what your disorder is, then the doctors, therapists, and group sessions will take care of the rest.

*An excerpt from healthconsciousinc.com

How the brain responds to positive thinking
'The brain's ability to change with repetition, called neuroplasticity, gives it the capacity to change over time. Neuroscience studies have shown that repetitive movement or behaviors grow brain matter, regardless of age. This also involves positive thinking: the more consistent positive thoughts, the more brain neurons change chemical signals, altering the structure and function of the brain associated with positive behavioral changes and healing. These changes can also be positive or negative depending on the consistency of behaviors, such as exercising daily or drug addiction, for example. The brain changes can go either way.'

In other words, what you do on a daily basis affects your brain. The activities you choose throughout each day affect what your brain picks up on and learns. From the moment you wake up in the morning, your brain is standing at attention waiting for orders. Waiting to absorb positive or negative thoughts and emotions. *You* can have control over what your brain absorbs. Whether you see it or not, know that you have control. Let that post-it note on your mirror be the first thing your brain absorbs each day. When that glass-half-empty thought enters your mind, fight it. Don't just sit there and take that mental beating. Respond to it! Defend yourself against it!

I can do this. I will be happy. Sour Skittles are awesome. That breeze feels great.

Anything positive that you notice, POINT IT OUT. Say it to yourself. The positive thought doesn't necessarily have to pertain to your recovery. It can be about anything. Just acknowledge it. Notice it. Enjoy the fact that you didn't burn the bacon.

Yes! Unburnt bacon!

That's a positive. Enjoy that positivity. Bring it into your life. Even if you aren't feeling it, bring it. Eventually, you will feel it and it will work wonders for you and your recovery. I promise you it will.

Do this as often as you can and your mind will pick up on it. Again, be patient. Your mind won't pick up on it right away. Give it some time. Eventually, your mind will naturally notice these things and they'll make you feel good without you having to force yourself to feel good about them. Be proactive in your recovery. You have to be involved to some extent. If you rely solely on just medications then I'm sorry to say that you are going to have a long and hard battle. You will need to work as well. It will require effort and lots of it. I know, you're mentally and emotionally exhausted. Effort from you is impossible right now. And that's okay. At the beginning of your treatment, that's fine. But you need to gradually include yourself over time within the treatment and recovery. A group therapy session on Tuesday. Positive thoughts on Wednesday. Take a break on Thursday. On Friday go for a thirty-minute walk. Start to do breathing exercises every other day the following week. Don't overwhelm yourself all at once. You've been overwhelmed for too long. The last thing you need to do is overwhelm yourself even more by doing too much to get better.

It's going to work out. I can do this. I will do this.

Ha! I just made you say something positive.

That's all it takes. And in the beginning, it doesn't matter whether you believe those positive thoughts or not. Most people don't. Most people with depression immediately think the opposite. They see the glass half empty. They see the negative because their mind is telling them to see the negative first. You've been living through so much negativity for so long that you wake up and expect it. You're not choosing to be negative in every aspect of your life. Your mind and the depression are choosing what you see and feel. You will get control of your thoughts. You will eventually see the glass half full instead of half empty. But it will take time to turn those thoughts around. So be patient with yourself.

"To lose patience is to lose the battle." - Mahatma Gandhi

Indiana

There have been several days throughout my recovery where I've awoken to racing, negative thoughts. How bad is my bipolar going to be today? How bad is the traffic going to be on my way to my appointment? How bad are the boys going to complain about doing their schoolwork today? How bad. How bad. How bad. Immediate negativity. I've been there. I've been at that place in life where every aspect of everything seems like it's at its worst. Nothing ever goes right. You've gotten caught in a pattern.

Being honest with yourself is something that will work wonders towards this particular part of your disorder. It will also help your overall recovery and treatment. If you have the ability to point out how bad everything might be that day, then you have the ability to see how good things might be that day. Yes, depression brings the worst thoughts to the front of your mind, but you still can recognize those positive thoughts, however few they may be. You most likely know that you're sad and depressed and may not be feeling like yourself. Being honest with yourself and telling yourself that something isn't right is key. It is a must. At some point, you have got to confront yourself and acknowledge what is going on. Being depressed and acknowledging your depression are two different things.

Those with severe, debilitating depression or mania might not be able to make this acknowledgment and will need outside help or inpatient care. At this moment I'm talking about those people that are still somewhat functioning on their own. Your mental state isn't great but you're getting up every day and trying to face the world. You know something isn't right. Recognizing it and being honest with yourself about what's going on will work wonders. This was the hardest part of my recovery and treatment. Telling myself that I had a problem and being honest with myself about what was going on inside my head.

In the beginning, when the manic episode took control, I didn't have the ability to think for myself. The disorder had complete control over everything I did. But as I started getting treatment here and there, I slowly regained the ability to think for myself and make proper decisions about things. But even as things improved, I still refused to be honest with myself about what I had been through, what I was going through, and most importantly, that I had a mental disability.

To this day, over twenty-one years since my diagnosis, I have not fully accepted the fact that I am bipolar. That my brain has a chemical imbalance and it can ignite at any moment and take complete control of every aspect of my life. How can anyone fully accept that? I've looked at myself in the mirror and tried my best to force words into the silhouette I see opposite of me.

You don't own me. You don't control me. You don't think for me.

No matter how many words I tried to force into that mirror, it never worked. I was refusing to let the disorder be a part of me. I would get so angry seeing my reflection each day. I wouldn't see me. I wouldn't see the freckles on my face. I wouldn't see my crooked nose or uneven ears. All I saw was a person with bipolar. I saw the person who was in control of my emotions and my thoughts. Until one day I looked in the mirror and was completely honest with myself and my disorder.

You are within me. You are a part of me. You are me.

I will be bipolar for the rest of my life. And if you're bipolar you will also be bipolar for the rest of your life. There is no way around it. There are two things you can do.

1. Give up and live a terrible life of depression and/or mania while struggling to find the tiniest of things in life that just might provide a few seconds of happiness and normalcy.
2. Be honest with yourself and accept that your disorder will always be a part of you and seek help and eventually gain some kind of control of your disorder and your life.

What you're experiencing is not going to just magically go away one day and forever cease to exist. Yes, you may have depression for months and then not experience it again for ten years. But the cause, if it's bipolar-related, will forever be seeded into the depths of your brain. Do you want to live with some control or no control at all? Do you want to put your body through the side effects of medications in exchange for mental relaxation? Do you want to spill your guts in front of a therapist or group of strangers who are going through the same things you're going through? Or, do you just want to relinquish control and deal with the worst when the worst arrives?

I chose medication. I chose group therapy. I chose to see a psychiatrist. I chose to be positive. I chose to accept my disorder. I chose to fight.

I hope you choose to fight as well.

West Virginia

I have relinquished control many times during my fight against mania and depression. I've accepted my disorder one day only to turn around and deny it the next. My recovery has taken years, and it's still in the works, but I am here. I have naturally happy moments instead of forced happiness to cover up whatever the disorder was trying to make me feel. It's not that I didn't want to be happy during those terrible episodes, it's that I wasn't allowed to be. I wasn't even allowed to be sad at certain times. At my worst mentally, I may as well have been in solitary confinement on death row. It feels like your mind is confined to the veins of the disorder that surround it. I've been in a therapist's office spilling my guts to the point that I ran out of words and ways to express how I was feeling. I've been so depressed that it felt like my brain stopped working. So depressed that I was scared of the next thought my mind would create, no matter what it was about. I've cried myself to sleep in the darkness and silence of a psychiatric unit. I tell you these things so you can see that it's not just you, that you're not alone. Life can go on. You can recover from those depths. You have fight in you. It's human nature to survive. The instincts to do so are in you. Find them and don't let go.

These days my disorder is managed really well, but I still do not have full control, and I never will. But I have accepted that. I've opened up and have been honest with myself about where I am. Who I am. And what I am. And doing so has led to a great, healthy life. I haven't touched drugs in many years. I can now spot symptoms and react to them in a healthy way instead of reaching for something to cover them up and ignore them. I hope one day you can face yourself and confront the disorder that may be holding you back. I hope you get to the point where you can realize that it's not you. I hope one day you can accept your diagnosis. I hope you can eventually accept the fact that you're not perfect, that no one is perfect, and that you shouldn't waste any more time or energy trying to be. You might be in a psychiatric ward right now reading this. I know how lonely it can be there. I know how lost and insignificant you can feel. I know how it feels to think that no one around you understands what you're trying to say or express. I've felt all of those things. I've risen from those depths. And you can as well. I know you can.

It *can* be done. I am living proof of that.

Mentally I was dealt a crap hand at life and I kept betting each round hoping for a turn of luck with the last card. That luck would never come until I accepted my disorder. Not only was I in denial, but I would complain about my disorder and what it had done to me to whoever would listen. I would even complain to myself. But why waste energy complaining when it accomplishes nothing? Recently, I've tried my best to stop living in the dark depths of the past and I hope you can do that at some point as well. Sure it's okay to look back on life.

But if you're looking back on negatives, try to turn them into positives, and learn from them. Bring that positivity into your life. Embrace it. You didn't burn the bacon! Pat yourself on the back. You went to a therapy session! That's a positive. Embrace it! Reward yourself for going to therapy with extra bacon the next morning. Be proactive with your treatment and recovery. Stay on top of things. If you falter, don't punish yourself. I didn't get to where I'm at today without taking any backward steps. I failed at things. I refused things. And I did those things many times. Learn from those moments. Don't let them define you or your recovery.

I sincerely hope that you are able to overcome whatever it is you may be going through. I hope you can acknowledge that it's not you, that it's something within you. I hope you can be patient with your recovery. I hope you learn during your recovery. I hope you find joy, happiness, and comfort. Most importantly, I hope you can conquer whatever it is that you're going through so that one day you too are able to find yourself. Find your purpose. Find your reason.

I've learned many things during my struggles with bipolar. I've learned how much fight I have inside of me during my lowest and hardest times. I've learned how dark life can get and that I never want to be there again. I've learned to be patient. I've learned I'm not owed anything. I've learned that I am bipolar and I always will be. I've learned I'm not perfect and I never will be. I've learned that no matter how bad my life may get, I was not put here to struggle. I was not put here to suffer. I've learned acceptance. I've learned to have faith in myself and faith in those helping me along the way. I've also learned my purpose. If I had never fought so hard against my disorders I don't believe I would have ever found my purpose in life. A higher power put me on this planet for a reason.

That reason wasn't to be a soldier in the Army. I wasn't put here to be a world leader or to save lives as a doctor. Nor was I put here to be a Hollywood celebrity or a world-famous athlete.

I was put here to be a father. I was put here to share my mental experiences and struggles with you, which I am more than happy to do. And I truly hope it helps you in some way. And I am more than content with being a father.

It may have taken until I was forty years old to come to this conclusion, but I finally found my purpose.

I found my reason.

I found Rhode Island.

Massachusetts

'Be True To You'
-Anonymous
As you set out on life's road
unsure of the path you'll go,
the most important thing you can do
is to always be true to you.
Always remember who you are
in moments of struggle or fear.
Never forget or give up on
the hopes and dreams you hold dear.
There will be setbacks and rejection
and moments of failure too,
but you must overcome any frustration
to achieve the potential of you.
Don't forget to smile, or laugh,
or to live in the present;
no matter where life takes you
make every memory pleasant.
As you travel along your journey,
know that you're never alone.
Be true to yourself,
and make yourself your home.

Vermont

'Personal Quest'
-Anonymous
For most of my life, I've been on a quest
To discover just who I might be,
Earnestly searching, day after day,
So desperate to recognize me.
I've felt moments of utter fulfillment
And moments I couldn't go on,
But I knew for the sake of my heart and my soul,
To succeed, I would have to be strong.
But the people around me seemed so lost themselves
That I feared I might be on my own.
But then there'd be someone who would reach out and help
And remind me I wasn't alone.
I've wanted so much to be happy,
To know what it was to feel peace,
And I thought if I finally felt sure of myself,
Then the pain and the struggles would cease.
But I've learned that this journey is endless;
The discoveries are fresh every day,
And no matter how much I might know of myself,
They'll be times I will still lose my way.

And as I've grown older, I truly believe
I may never know all I can be.
But the answers are not waiting out in the world
But have always laid right inside me.
We're all on this quest to discover ourselves,
Together but through our own ways,
Overcoming whatever might get in our paths,
So we can feel better someday.
But always remember not to stray far
From what matters and what's really true.
In this life you don't have to be perfect.
In the end, you just have to be you.

Minnesota

What matters most is not what's behind us or before us, but
what is within us.
-Ralph Waldo Emerson

Where you are is not who you are.
-Unknown

It's okay to not be okay.
-Unknown

There is hope, even when your brain tells you there isn't.
-John Green

You don't have to control your thoughts.
You just have to stop letting them control you.
-Dan Millman

Mental health is not a destination, but a process.
It's about how you drive, not where you're going.
- Noam Shpancer, PhD

You are not your illness. You have an individual story to tell.
You have a name, a history, a personality. Staying yourself is
part of the battle.
-Julian Seifter

Just because no one else can heal or do your inner work for
you doesn't mean you can, should, or need to do it alone."
- Lisa Olivera

Kentucky

Still I'll rise.
-Maya Angelou

Rhode Island

Help And Thanks

I f you need someone to talk to about what you may be going through please do not hesitate to contact me.

jstevenhughes@gmail.com

Or dial 988, which is the Suicide & Crisis Hotline

1-800-662-4357 Substance Abuse & Mental Health Services Administration

mentalhealthhotline.org 1-866-903-3787

crisistextline.org Text 'home' to 741741

1-833-852-6262 For mental health assistance during and after pregnancy

If by chance you are one of the 'anonymous' people that wrote one of the poems or quotes in the back of the book please feel free to contact about the usage of your wonderful words.

I want to say thank you to my family. I love you all so much.

Special thanks to my mother for all she did from a judicial standpoint to help me. And even more thanks to her for providing the foreword of this book. Thank you to the mental health providers of Fort Roots Veteran's Hospital in North Little Rock, AR. Thanks to those that helped me at the state hospital and the Fort Bliss, TX psychiatric unit. Thanks to my mother and stepfather for also opening up their home to me and my children and for helping to raise and take care of them. Thanks to my ex wife for opening up her home to me. Thanks to the Lonoke County Housing Authority for providing me shelter when I was at my lowest point in life. Thanks to my sons. You are the greatest sons a father could ask for. I couldn't have asked for a better purpose in life. Thanks to all for taking the time to read this. I wish you all the best.

Sincerely,

Jeremy S. Hughes

Information

Bipolar disorder is a mental illness that causes unusual shifts in a person's mood, energy, activity levels, and concentration. These shifts can make it difficult to carry out day-to-day tasks. Bipolar disorder is often diagnosed during late adolescence (teen years) or early adulthood. Sometimes, bipolar symptoms can appear in children. Although the symptoms may vary over time, bipolar disorder usually requires lifelong treatment. Following a prescribed treatment plan can help people manage their symptoms and improve their quality of life.

Symptoms
Depression

During a period of depression, your symptoms may include:

- feeling sad, hopeless or irritable most of the time
- lacking energy
- difficulty concentrating and remembering things
- loss of interest in everyday activities
- feelings of emptiness or worthlessness
- feelings of guilt and despair
- feeling pessimistic about everything

- self-doubt
- being delusional, having hallucinations and disturbed or illogical thinking
- lack of appetite
- difficulty sleeping
- waking up early
- suicidal thoughts

Mania
The manic phase of bipolar disorder may include:

- feeling very happy, elated or overjoyed
- talking very quickly
- feeling full of energy
- feeling self-important
- feeling full of great new ideas and having important plans
- being easily distracted
- being easily irritated or agitated
- being delusional, having hallucinations and disturbed or illogical thinking
- not feeling like sleeping
- doing things that often have disastrous consequences – such as spending large sums of money on expensive and sometimes unaffordable items
- making decisions or saying things that are out of character and that others see as being risky or harmful

You know your body and mind more than anyone. If it feels like something is wrong, something is most likely wrong. Please don't hesitate to take care of yourself.